# GLOBAL INVESTMENT PERFORMANCE STANDARDS (GIPS®) FOR FIRMS

2020

CFA Institute®
Global Investment
Performance Standards

ISBN 978-1-942713-71-5

# CONTENTS

# PREFACE

CFA Institute is a global not-for-profit association of investment professionals with the mission of leading the investment profession globally by setting the highest standards of ethics, education, and professional excellence. CFA Institute has a longstanding history of commitment to establishing and supporting the Global Investment Performance Standards (GIPS®). The GIPS standards are ethical standards for calculating and presenting investment performance based on the principles of fair representation and full disclosure.

The GIPS standards are the recognized standard for calculating and presenting investment performance around the world. Compliance with the GIPS standards has become a firm's "passport" to market investment management services globally. Asset owners that comply demonstrate a commitment to adhering to global best practices. As of June 2019, CFA Institute has partnered with organizations in more than 40 countries and regions that contribute to the development and promotion of the GIPS standards.

## History

- In 1995, CFA Institute, formerly known as the Association for Investment Management and Research (AIMR), sponsored and funded the Global Investment Performance Standards Committee to develop global standards for calculating and presenting investment performance, based on the existing AIMR Performance Presentation Standards (AIMR-PPS®).
- The first Global Investment Performance Standards were published in April 1999. That year, the Global Investment Performance Standards Committee was replaced by the Investment Performance Council (IPC) to further develop and promote the GIPS standards. The development of the GIPS standards was a global industry initiative with participation from individuals and organizations from more than 15 countries.
- The IPC was charged with developing provisions for other asset classes (e.g., real estate and private equity) and addressing other performance-related issues (e.g., fees and advertising) to broaden the scope and applicability of the GIPS standards. The second edition of the GIPS standards, published in February 2005, accomplished this goal.
- With the 2005 edition release and the growing adoption and expansion of the GIPS standards, the IPC decided to move to a single global investment performance standard that would eliminate the need for local variations of the GIPS standards. All country-specific performance standards converged with the GIPS standards, resulting in 25 countries adopting a single, global standard for the calculation and presentation of investment performance.

- In 2005, with the convergence of country-specific versions to the GIPS standards and the need to reorganize the governance structure to facilitate involvement from GIPS Standards Sponsors, CFA Institute dissolved the IPC and created the GIPS Executive Committee and the GIPS Council. The GIPS Executive Committee served as the decision-making authority for the GIPS standards, and the GIPS Council facilitated the involvement of all GIPS Standards Sponsors in the ongoing development and promotion of the GIPS standards.
- In 2008, the GIPS Executive Committee began a review of the GIPS standards in an effort to further refine the provisions. The GIPS Executive Committee collaborated closely with its technical subcommittees, specially formed working groups, and GIPS Standards Sponsors. These groups reviewed the existing provisions and guidance and conducted surveys and other research in the effort to produce the 2010 edition of the GIPS standards.
- In 2017, the GIPS Executive Committee concluded that the GIPS standards should better accommodate the needs of managers of pooled funds and alternative investments, as well as firms focusing on high-net-worth clients. In 2017, a Consultation Paper, which described the proposed key concepts of the GIPS standards and requested feedback on specific issues, was issued for public comment. The public comments received generally supported the proposed concepts. Subsequently, the 2020 GIPS Standards Exposure Draft was released on 31 August 2018. The final version of the 2020 edition of the GIPS standards was issued on 30 June 2019.
- The GIPS standards were originally created for investment firms managing composite strategies, with a focus on how firms present performance of composites to prospective clients. Asset owners, who were always able to claim compliance if they had discretion over their assets, struggled to understand how the GIPS standards applied to them. To address asset owners' needs, in 2014 the Guidance Statement on the Application of the GIPS Standards to Asset Owners was issued. This Guidance Statement explained how the requirements of the GIPS standards did or did not apply to asset owners. In the 2020 edition, separate provisions were created so that firms and asset owners each have provisions designed for them. Firms and those asset owners that market their services must follow the GIPS Standards for Firms. Asset owners that do not market their services will follow the GIPS Standards for Asset Owners. The GIPS Standards for Verifiers explain the procedures a verifier must follow when conducting a verification or performance examination.

  

# INTRODUCTION

## Preamble—Why Is a Global Investment Performance Standard Needed?

**Standardize Investment Performance:** Financial markets and the investment management industry have become increasingly global in nature. The growth in the types and number of financial entities, the globalization of the investment process, and the increased competition among investment management firms all demonstrate the need to standardize the calculation and presentation of investment performance.

**Global Passport:** Asset managers and both existing and prospective clients benefit from an established global standard for calculating and presenting investment performance. Investment practices, regulation, performance measurement, and reporting of performance vary considerably from country to country. By adhering to a global standard, firms in countries with minimal or no investment performance standards can compete for business on an equal footing with firms from countries with more-developed standards. Firms from countries with established practices can have more confidence in being fairly compared with local firms when competing for business in countries that have not previously adopted performance standards. Performance standards that are accepted globally enable investment firms to measure and present their investment performance so that investors can readily compare investment performance among firms.

**Investor Confidence:** Organizations that adhere to investment performance standards help assure investors and beneficiaries that the firm's and the asset owner's investment performance is complete and fairly presented. Both prospective and existing clients of investment firms as well as asset owner oversight bodies benefit from a global investment performance standard by having a greater degree of confidence in the performance information presented to them.

## Mission and Objectives

The mission of the GIPS standards is to promote ethics and integrity and instill trust through the use of the GIPS standards by achieving universal demand for compliance by asset owners, adoption by asset managers, and support from regulators for the ultimate benefit of the global investment community.

The objectives of the GIPS standards are as follows:

- Promote investor interests and instill investor confidence.
- Ensure accurate and consistent data.

- Obtain worldwide acceptance of a single standard for calculating and presenting performance.
- Promote fair, global competition among investment firms.
- Promote industry self-regulation on a global basis.

## Overview

Key concepts of the GIPS standards that apply to firms include the following:

- The GIPS standards are ethical standards for investment performance presentation to ensure fair representation and full disclosure of investment performance.
- Meeting the objectives of fair representation and full disclosure is likely to require more than simply adhering to the minimum requirements of the GIPS standards. Firms should also adhere to the recommendations to achieve best practice in the calculation and presentation of performance.
- Firms must comply with all applicable requirements of the GIPS standards, including any Guidance Statements, interpretations, and Questions & Answers (Q&As) published by CFA Institute and the GIPS standards governing bodies.
- The GIPS standards do not address every aspect of performance measurement and will continue to evolve over time to address additional areas of investment performance.
- The GIPS standards require firms to create and maintain composites for all strategies for which the firm manages segregated accounts or markets to segregated accounts. Firms must include all actual, fee-paying, discretionary segregated accounts in at least one composite defined by investment mandate, objective, or strategy. Pooled funds must also be included in any composite for which the pooled fund meets the composite definition. Firms must maintain and make available information about all of the strategies they manage using composites or pooled funds. These requirements prevent firms from cherry-picking their best performance.
- The GIPS standards rely on the integrity of input data, the quality of which is critical to creating accurate performance presentations. The underlying valuations of portfolio holdings drive performance. It is essential for these and other inputs to be accurate. The GIPS standards require firms to adhere to certain calculation methodologies to allow for comparability across firms.

  

## Historical Performance Record

A firm is required to initially present, at a minimum, five years of annual investment performance that is compliant with the GIPS standards. If the composite or pooled fund has been in existence less than five years, the firm must present performance since the composite or pooled fund inception date. Prospectively, the firm must present an additional year of performance each year, building up to a minimum of 10 years of GIPS-compliant performance.

Firms may link non-GIPS-compliant performance to their GIPS-compliant performance provided that only GIPS-compliant performance is presented for periods after the minimum effective compliance date, which differs depending on the asset type:

- 1 January 2006 for real estate and private equity composites and pooled funds, as well as wrap fee composites.
- 1 January 2000 for all other composites and pooled funds.

## Claiming Compliance and Verification

Firms must take all steps necessary to ensure that they have satisfied all the applicable requirements of the GIPS standards before claiming compliance. Firms are strongly encouraged to perform periodic internal compliance checks. Implementing adequate internal controls during all stages of the investment performance process—from data input to preparing GIPS Composite Reports and GIPS Pooled Fund Reports—instills confidence in the validity of performance presented as well as in the claim of compliance.

Firms may choose to have an independent third-party verification. Verification is a process by which a verification firm (verifier) conducts testing of a firm on a firm-wide basis in accordance with the required verification procedures of the GIPS standards. Verification provides assurance on whether the firm's policies and procedures related to composite and pooled fund maintenance, as well as the calculation, presentation, and distribution of performance, have been designed in compliance with the GIPS standards and have been implemented on a firm-wide basis. The value of verification is widely recognized, and being verified is considered to be best practice. It is strongly recommended that firms be verified. In addition to verification, firms may also choose to have specifically focused testing of a composite or pooled fund (performance examination) performed by an independent third-party verifier to provide additional assurance regarding the performance of a particular composite or pooled fund.

## Implementing a Global Standard

One objective of the GIPS standards is to obtain worldwide acceptance of a single standard for the calculation and presentation of investment performance in a fair and comparable format that provides full disclosure. To facilitate the implementation of the GIPS standards, CFA Institute, together with the GIPS standards governing bodies, creates and administers the GIPS standards while local GIPS Standards Sponsors help to promote them.

Countries without an investment performance standard are strongly encouraged to promote the GIPS standards as the local standard and translate them into the local language when necessary. Although the GIPS standards may be translated into many languages, if a discrepancy arises, the English version of the GIPS standards is the official governing version.

The self-regulatory nature of the GIPS standards necessitates a strong commitment to ethical integrity. Self-regulation also assists regulators in exercising their responsibility for ensuring the fair disclosure of information within financial markets. Regulators are encouraged to do the following:

- Recognize the benefit of voluntary compliance with standards that represent global best practices;
- Consider taking enforcement action against firms that falsely claim compliance with the GIPS standards; and
- Recognize the value of and encourage independent third-party verification.

Where existing laws, regulations, or industry standards already impose requirements related to the calculation and presentation of investment performance, firms are strongly encouraged to comply with the GIPS standards in addition to applicable regulatory requirements. Compliance with applicable laws and regulations does not necessarily lead to compliance with the GIPS standards. In cases in which laws and/or regulations conflict with the GIPS standards, firms are required to comply with the laws and regulations and make full disclosure of the conflict in the GIPS Report.

## GIPS Standards Sponsors

The presence of a local GIPS Standards Sponsor is essential for effective implementation of the GIPS standards and ongoing support within a country or region. Working in partnership with CFA Institute, GIPS Standards Sponsors play a key role in promoting the GIPS standards globally. GIPS Standards Sponsors, composed of one or more industry organizations, provide an important link between their local markets and the GIPS standards governing bodies. In addition to delivering educational programs and promoting the GIPS standards across the local investment profession, the GIPS Standards Sponsors own any CFA Institute-approved translation of the GIPS standards materials and are responsible for protecting it.

  

**Endorsed GIPS Standards Sponsors** (as of 30 June 2019)

**Australia**
Financial Services Council (FSC)

**Canada**
Canadian Investment Performance Council (CIPC)

**China**
CFA Society Beijing

**Cyprus**
CFA Society Cyprus

**Czech Republic**
CFA Society Czech Republic and Czech Capital Market Association (AKAT)

**Denmark**
CFA Society Denmark and The Danish Finance Society

**France**
CFA Society France and Association Française de la Gestion Financière (AFG)

**Germany**
German Asset Management Standards Committee (GAMSC):
Bundesverband Investment und Asset Manager e.V. (BVI); Deutsche Vereinigung fur Finanzanalyse und Assetment Management (DVFA); and CFA Society Germany

**Ghana**
Ghana Securities Industry Association (GSIA)

**Greece**
CFA Society Greece

**India**
CFA Society India

**Indonesia**
CFA Society Indonesia and Indonesia Association of Mutual Fund Managers (Asosiasi Pengelola Reksa Dana Indonesia, or APRDI)

**Ireland**
Irish Association of Investment Managers (IAIM)

**Italy**
Italian Investment Performance Committee (IIPC):
Associazione Bancaria Italiana (ABI); Associazione Italiana degli Analisti e Consulenti Finanziari (AIAF); Assogestioni; Società per lo sviluppo del Mercato dei Fondi Pensione (Mefop); Associazione Italiana Revisori Contabili (Assirevi); and CFA Society Italy

**Japan**
The Securities Analysts Association of Japan (SAAJ)

**Kazakhstan**
Association of Financial and Investment Analysts (AFIA)

**Korea**
Korea Investment Performance Committee (KIPC)

**Liechtenstein**
Liechtenstein Bankers Association (LBA)

**Mexico**
CFA Society Mexico

**Micronesia**
Asia Pacific Association for Fiduciary Studies (APAFS)

**The Netherlands**
VBA-Beleggingsprofessionals

**New Zealand**
CFA Society New Zealand

**Nigeria**
Nigeria Investment Performance Committee: CFA Society Nigeria; Pensions Operators Association of Nigeria (PENOP); and Fund Managers Association of Nigeria (FMAN)

**Norway**
The Norwegian Society of Financial Analysts (NFF)

**Pakistan**
CFA Society Pakistan

**Peru**
Procapitales

**Philippines**
CFA Society Philippines; Fund Managers Association of the Philippines (FMAP); and Trust Officers Association of the Philippines (TOAP)

**Poland**
CFA Society Poland

**Portugal**
Associação Portuguesa de Analista Financeiros (APAF)

**Russia**
CFA Association Russia

**Saudi Arabia**
CFA Society Saudi Arabia

**Singapore**
Investment Management Association of Singapore (IMAS)

**South Africa**
Association for Savings and Investment South Africa (ASISA)

**Spain**
Asociación Española de Presentación de Resultados de Gestión

**Sri Lanka**
CFA Society Sri Lanka

**Sweden**
CFA Society Sweden and The Swedish Society of Financial Analysts (Sveriges Finansanalytikers Forening, or SFF)

**Switzerland**
Swiss Funds & Asset Management Association (SFAMA)

**Thailand**
The Association of Provident Fund (AOP)

**Ukraine**
The Ukrainian Association of Investment Business (UAIB)

**United Kingdom**
United Kingdom Investment Performance Committee (UKIPC):
The Investment Association (TIA);
The Association of British Insurers (ABI);
Pensions and Lifetime Savings Association (PLSA); The Association of Consulting Actuaries (ACA); The Society of Pension Consultants (SPC); The Investment Property Forum (IPF); The Alternative Investment Management Association (AIMA); and
The Wealth Management Association (WMA)

**United States**
United States Investment Performance Committee (USIPC) of CFA Institute

  

## Provisions of the Global Investment Performance Standards

The 2020 Edition of the GIPS Standards has three chapters:

1) GIPS Standards for Firms
2) GIPS Standards for Asset Owners
3) GIPS Standards for Verifiers

Organizations that compete for business must comply with the GIPS Standards for Firms.

The GIPS Standards for Firms are divided into the following eight sections:

1) **Fundamentals of Compliance:** Several core principles create the foundation for the GIPS standards, including properly defining the firm, providing GIPS Reports to all prospective clients and prospective pooled fund investors, adhering to applicable laws and regulations, and ensuring that information presented is not false or misleading. Two important issues that a firm must consider when becoming compliant with the GIPS standards are the definition of the firm and the firm's definition of discretion. The definition of the firm is the foundation for firm-wide compliance and creates defined boundaries whereby total firm assets can be determined. The firm's definition of discretion establishes criteria to judge which portfolios must be included in a composite and is based on the firm's ability to implement its investment strategies.
2) **Input Data and Calculation Methodology:** Consistency of input data used to calculate performance is critical to effective compliance with the GIPS standards and establishes the foundation for full, fair, and comparable investment performance presentations. Achieving comparability among investment management firms' performance presentations requires uniformity in methods used to calculate returns. The GIPS standards mandate the use of certain calculation methodologies to facilitate comparability.
3) **Composite and Pooled Fund Maintenance:** A composite is an aggregation of one or more portfolios managed according to a similar investment mandate, objective, or strategy. The composite return is the asset-weighted average of the performance of all portfolios in the composite. Creating meaningful composites is essential to the fair presentation, consistency, and comparability of performance over time and among firms. Pooled funds must be included in composites if they meet a composite definition.

**Reporting Sections:** These four sections detail the requirements and recommendations for reporting the following types of returns:

4) **Composite Time-Weighted Return Report**
5) **Composite Money-Weighted Return Report**
6) **Pooled Fund Time-Weighted Return Report**
7) **Pooled Fund Money-Weighted Return Report.**

  

Each of the four reporting sections is self-contained and includes requirements and recommendations relevant to that particular report. Firms must include the information from the respective section depending on whether they are preparing a composite or a pooled fund report, as well as on whether time-weighted returns or money-weighted returns are included.

After constructing the composites, gathering the input data, and calculating returns, the firm must incorporate this information in GIPS Reports based on the requirements in the GIPS standards for presenting investment performance. No finite set of requirements can cover all potential situations or anticipate future developments in investment industry structure, technology, products, or practices. When appropriate, firms have the responsibility to include in GIPS Reports information not addressed by the GIPS standards.

Disclosures allow firms to elaborate on the data provided in the presentation and give the reader the proper context in which to understand the performance. To comply with the GIPS standards, firms must disclose certain information in all GIPS Reports regarding their performance and the policies adopted by the firm. Although some disclosures are required for all firms, others are specific to certain circumstances and may not be applicable in all situations. Firms are not required to make negative assurance disclosures (e.g., if the firm does not use leverage in a particular composite strategy, no disclosure of the use of leverage is required). One of the essential disclosures for every firm is the claim of compliance. Once a firm meets all the applicable requirements of the GIPS standards, it must appropriately use the claim of compliance to indicate compliance with the GIPS standards. Firms are also required to submit a GIPS Compliance Notification Form to CFA Institute when they initially claim compliance and on an annual basis thereafter.

8) **GIPS Advertising Guidelines:** Firms are not required to follow the GIPS Advertising Guidelines when creating an advertisement, but if they would like to claim compliance with the GIPS standards in an advertisement, they must adhere to the GIPS Advertising Guidelines or include a GIPS Report.

**Glossary:** Words appearing in small capital letters in Sections 1–8 are defined terms. The Glossary includes a description of each defined term.

**Appendices:** The appendices include samples of GIPS Reports, lists of composites and pooled fund descriptions, and GIPS Advertisements.

  

# EFFECTIVE DATE

The effective date for the 2020 edition of the GIPS standards is 1 January 2020. GIPS Reports that include performance for periods ending on or after 31 December 2020 must be prepared in accordance with the 2020 edition of the GIPS standards. Prior editions of the GIPS standards may be found on the CFA Institute website (www.cfainstitute.org).

# 1. FUNDAMENTALS OF COMPLIANCE

## 1.A. Fundamentals of Compliance—Requirements

1.A.1 The GIPS standards MUST be applied on a FIRM-wide basis. Compliance MUST be met on a FIRM-wide basis and cannot be met on a COMPOSITE, POOLED FUND, or PORTFOLIO basis.

1.A.2 The FIRM MUST be defined as an investment firm, subsidiary, or division held out to the public as a DISTINCT BUSINESS ENTITY.

1.A.3 To initially claim compliance with the GIPS standards, the FIRM MUST attain compliance for a minimum of five years or for the period since the FIRM inception if the FIRM has been in existence for less than five years.

1.A.4 The FIRM MUST comply with all applicable REQUIREMENTS of the GIPS standards, including any Guidance Statements, interpretations, and Questions & Answers (Q&As) published by CFA Institute and the GIPS standards governing bodies.

1.A.5 The FIRM MUST:

a. Document its policies and procedures used in establishing and maintaining compliance with the REQUIREMENTS of the GIPS standards, as well as any RECOMMENDATIONS it has chosen to adopt, and apply them consistently.

b. Create policies and procedures to monitor and identify changes and additions to all of the Guidance Statements, interpretations, and Q&As published by CFA Institute and the GIPS standards governing bodies.

1.A.6 The FIRM MUST:

a. Comply with all applicable laws and regulations regarding the calculation and presentation of performance.

b. Create policies and procedures to monitor and identify changes and additions to laws and regulations regarding the calculation and presentation of performance.

1.A.7 The FIRM MUST NOT present performance or PERFORMANCE-RELATED INFORMATION that is false or misleading. This REQUIREMENT applies to all performance or PERFORMANCE-RELATED INFORMATION on a FIRM-wide basis and is not limited to those materials that reference the GIPS standards. The FIRM may provide any performance or PERFORMANCE-RELATED INFORMATION that is specifically requested by a PROSPECTIVE CLIENT or PROSPECTIVE INVESTOR for use in a one-on-one presentation.

1.A.8 If the FIRM does not meet all the applicable REQUIREMENTS of the GIPS standards, the FIRM MUST NOT represent or state that it is "in compliance with the Global Investment Performance Standards except for..." or make any other statements that may indicate compliance or partial compliance with the GIPS standards.

  

**1.A.9** Statements referring to the calculation methodology as being "in accordance," "in compliance," or "consistent" with the Global Investment Performance Standards, or similar statements, are prohibited.

**1.A.10** The FIRM MUST NOT make statements referring to the performance of a current client or POOLED FUND investor as being "calculated in accordance with the Global Investment Performance Standards," except for when a GIPS-compliant FIRM reports the performance of a SEGREGATED ACCOUNT to current clients or a POOLED FUND to current investors.

**1.A.11** The FIRM MUST make every reasonable effort to provide a GIPS COMPOSITE REPORT to all PROSPECTIVE CLIENTS when they initially become PROSPECTIVE CLIENTS. The FIRM MUST NOT choose to which PROSPECTIVE CLIENTS it presents a GIPS COMPOSITE REPORT.

**1.A.12** Once the FIRM has provided a GIPS COMPOSITE REPORT to a PROSPECTIVE CLIENT, the FIRM MUST provide an updated GIPS COMPOSITE REPORT at least once every 12 months if the PROSPECTIVE CLIENT is still a PROSPECTIVE CLIENT.

**1.A.13** The FIRM MUST make every reasonable effort to provide a GIPS REPORT to all LIMITED DISTRIBUTION POOLED FUND PROSPECTIVE INVESTORS when they initially become PROSPECTIVE INVESTORS. The GIPS REPORT may be either:

- **a.** A GIPS POOLED FUND REPORT, or
- **b.** A GIPS COMPOSITE REPORT. A GIPS COMPOSITE REPORT may be provided only if the LIMITED DISTRIBUTION POOLED FUND is included in the respective COMPOSITE.

The FIRM MUST NOT choose to which LIMITED DISTRIBUTION POOLED FUND PROSPECTIVE INVESTORS it presents a GIPS REPORT.

**1.A.14** Once the FIRM has provided a GIPS POOLED FUND REPORT or a GIPS COMPOSITE REPORT to a LIMITED DISTRIBUTION POOLED FUND PROSPECTIVE INVESTOR, the FIRM MUST provide an updated GIPS POOLED FUND REPORT or GIPS COMPOSITE REPORT at least once every 12 months if the LIMITED DISTRIBUTION POOLED FUND PROSPECTIVE INVESTOR is still a LIMITED DISTRIBUTION POOLED FUND PROSPECTIVE INVESTOR.

**1.A.15** The FIRM may provide a GIPS POOLED FUND REPORT or a GIPS COMPOSITE REPORT that includes the BROAD DISTRIBUTION POOLED FUND to BROAD DISTRIBUTION POOLED FUND PROSPECTIVE INVESTORS but is not REQUIRED to do so.

**1.A.16** When providing GIPS REPORTS to PROSPECTIVE CLIENTS and PROSPECTIVE INVESTORS, the FIRM MUST update these reports to include information through the most recent annual period end within 12 months of that annual period end.

**1.A.17** The FIRM MUST be able to demonstrate how it made every reasonable effort to provide:

- **a.** A GIPS COMPOSITE REPORT to those PROSPECTIVE CLIENTS REQUIRED to receive a GIPS COMPOSITE REPORT.
- **b.** A GIPS POOLED FUND REPORT or GIPS COMPOSITE REPORT to those LIMITED DISTRIBUTION POOLED FUND PROSPECTIVE INVESTORS REQUIRED to receive a GIPS POOLED FUND REPORT or GIPS COMPOSITE REPORT.

  

1.A.18 A COMPOSITE BENCHMARK used in a GIPS COMPOSITE REPORT MUST reflect the investment mandate, objective, or strategy of the COMPOSITE. The FIRM MUST NOT use a price-only BENCHMARK in a GIPS COMPOSITE REPORT.

1.A.19 A POOLED FUND BENCHMARK used in a GIPS POOLED FUND REPORT MUST reflect the investment mandate, objective, or strategy of the POOLED FUND. The FIRM MUST NOT use a price-only BENCHMARK in a GIPS POOLED FUND REPORT.

1.A.20 The FIRM MUST correct MATERIAL ERRORS in GIPS COMPOSITE REPORTS and MUST:

a. Provide the corrected GIPS COMPOSITE REPORT to the current verifier.

b. Provide the corrected GIPS COMPOSITE REPORT to current clients and any former verifiers that received the GIPS COMPOSITE REPORT that had the MATERIAL ERROR.

c. Make every reasonable effort to provide the corrected GIPS COMPOSITE REPORT to all current PROSPECTIVE CLIENTS and PROSPECTIVE INVESTORS that received the GIPS COMPOSITE REPORT that had the MATERIAL ERROR. The FIRM is not REQUIRED to provide the corrected GIPS COMPOSITE REPORT to former clients, former investors, former PROSPECTIVE CLIENTS, or former PROSPECTIVE INVESTORS.

1.A.21 The FIRM MUST correct MATERIAL ERRORS in GIPS POOLED FUND REPORTS and MUST:

a. Provide the corrected GIPS POOLED FUND REPORT to the current verifier.

b. Provide the corrected GIPS POOLED FUND REPORT to current investors and any former verifiers that received the GIPS POOLED FUND REPORT that had the MATERIAL ERROR.

c. Make every reasonable effort to provide the corrected GIPS POOLED FUND REPORT to all current PROSPECTIVE INVESTORS that received the GIPS POOLED FUND REPORT that had the MATERIAL ERROR. The FIRM is not REQUIRED to provide the corrected GIPS COMPOSITE REPORT to former investors or former PROSPECTIVE INVESTORS.

1.A.22 The FIRM MUST maintain:

a. A complete list of COMPOSITE DESCRIPTIONS. The FIRM MUST include terminated COMPOSITES on this list for at least five years after the COMPOSITE TERMINATION DATE.

b. A complete list of POOLED FUND DESCRIPTIONS for LIMITED DISTRIBUTION POOLED FUNDS. The FIRM is not REQUIRED to include terminated LIMITED DISTRIBUTION POOLED FUNDS on this list.

c. A complete list of BROAD DISTRIBUTION POOLED FUNDS. The FIRM is not REQUIRED to include terminated BROAD DISTRIBUTION POOLED FUNDS on this list.

1.A.23 The FIRM MUST provide:

a. The complete list of COMPOSITE DESCRIPTIONS to any PROSPECTIVE CLIENT that makes such a request.

b. The complete list of POOLED FUND DESCRIPTIONS for LIMITED DISTRIBUTION POOLED FUNDS to any LIMITED DISTRIBUTION POOLED FUND PROSPECTIVE

  

INVESTOR that makes such a request. This list may include only the LIMITED DISTRIBUTION POOLED FUNDS for which the PROSPECTIVE INVESTOR is eligible.

c. The complete list of BROAD DISTRIBUTION POOLED FUNDS to any BROAD DISTRIBUTION POOLED FUND PROSPECTIVE INVESTOR that makes such a request. This list may include only the BROAD DISTRIBUTION POOLED FUNDS for which the PROSPECTIVE INVESTOR is eligible. If the FIRM maintains a complete list of BROAD DISTRIBUTION POOLED FUNDS on its website, the FIRM may instead direct the PROSPECTIVE INVESTOR to the FIRM'S website.

d. The POOLED FUND DESCRIPTION for any BROAD DISTRIBUTION POOLED FUND to any BROAD DISTRIBUTION POOLED FUND PROSPECTIVE INVESTOR that makes such a request.

**1.A.24** The FIRM MUST provide:

a. A GIPS COMPOSITE REPORT for any COMPOSITE listed on the FIRM'S list of COMPOSITE DESCRIPTIONS to any PROSPECTIVE CLIENT that makes such a request.

b. A GIPS POOLED FUND REPORT or GIPS COMPOSITE REPORT, provided the LIMITED DISTRIBUTION POOLED FUND is included in the respective COMPOSITE, for any LIMITED DISTRIBUTION POOLED FUND on the FIRM'S list of POOLED FUND DESCRIPTIONS to any LIMITED DISTRIBUTION POOLED FUND PROSPECTIVE INVESTOR that makes such a request.

**1.A.25** All data and information necessary to support all items included in GIPS COMPOSITE REPORTS, GIPS POOLED FUND REPORTS, and GIPS ADVERTISEMENTS MUST be captured, maintained, and available within a reasonable time frame, for all periods presented in these reports and advertisements.

**1.A.26** The FIRM is responsible for its claim of compliance with the GIPS standards and MUST ensure that the records and information provided by any third party on which the FIRM relies meet the REQUIREMENTS of the GIPS standards.

**1.A.27** The FIRM MUST NOT LINK actual performance to historical THEORETICAL PERFORMANCE.

**1.A.28** Changes in the FIRM'S organization MUST NOT lead to alteration of historical performance.

**1.A.29** For TIME-WEIGHTED RETURNS presented in GIPS REPORTS, the FIRM MUST NOT LINK non-GIPS-compliant performance for periods beginning on or after the MINIMUM EFFECTIVE COMPLIANCE DATE to GIPS-compliant performance. The FIRM may LINK non-GIPS-compliant performance to GIPS-compliant performance in GIPS REPORTS provided that only GIPS-compliant performance is presented for periods beginning on or after the MINIMUM EFFECTIVE COMPLIANCE DATE.

**1.A.30** For MONEY-WEIGHTED RETURNS presented in GIPS REPORTS, the FIRM MUST NOT present non-GIPS-compliant performance for periods ending on or after the MINIMUM EFFECTIVE COMPLIANCE DATE. The FIRM may present non-GIPS-compliant performance in GIPS REPORTS for periods ending prior to the MINIMUM EFFECTIVE COMPLIANCE DATE.

  

1.A.31 When the FIRM jointly markets with other firms, the FIRM claiming compliance with the GIPS standards MUST ensure that the FIRM is clearly defined and separate relative to other firms being marketed and also that it is clear which FIRM is claiming compliance.

1.A.32 Performance from a past firm or affiliation may be used to represent the historical performance of the new or acquiring FIRM and LINKED to the performance of the new or acquiring FIRM if the new or acquiring FIRM meets the following REQUIREMENTS on a COMPOSITE-specific or POOLED FUND–specific basis:

a. Substantially all of the investment decision makers MUST be employed by the new or acquiring FIRM (e.g., research department staff, portfolio managers, and other relevant staff);

b. The decision-making process MUST remain substantially intact and independent within the new or acquiring FIRM;

c. The new or acquiring FIRM MUST have records to support the performance; and

d. There MUST be no break in the track record between the past firm or affiliation and the new or acquiring FIRM.

If any of the above REQUIREMENTS are not met, the performance from a past firm or affiliation MUST NOT be LINKED to the ongoing performance record of the new or acquiring FIRM.

1.A.33 Performance from a past firm or affiliation may be used to represent the historical performance of the new or acquiring FIRM when there is a break in the track record between the past firm or affiliation and the new or acquiring FIRM if the new or acquiring FIRM meets the following REQUIREMENTS on a COMPOSITE-specific or POOLED FUND–specific basis:

a. Substantially all of the investment decision makers MUST be employed by the new or acquiring FIRM (e.g., research department staff, portfolio managers, and other relevant staff);

b. The decision-making process MUST remain substantially intact and independent within the new or acquiring FIRM;

c. The new or acquiring FIRM MUST have records to support the performance;

d. The new or acquiring FIRM MUST separately present the performance before the break and after the break; and

e. The new or acquiring FIRM MUST NOT LINK performance prior to the break in the track record to the performance after the break in the track record.

1.A.34 If the FIRM acquires another firm or affiliation, the FIRM has one year to bring any non-compliant assets into compliance. Assets of the acquired non-compliant firm or affiliation MUST meet all the REQUIREMENTS of the GIPS standards within one year of the acquisition date, on a going forward basis.

1.A.35 The FIRM MUST present TIME-WEIGHTED RETURNS unless certain criteria are met, in which case the FIRM may present MONEY-WEIGHTED RETURNS. The FIRM may present

  

MONEY-WEIGHTED RETURNS only if the FIRM has control over the EXTERNAL CASH FLOWS into the PORTFOLIOS in the COMPOSITE or POOLED FUND and the PORTFOLIOS in the COMPOSITE have or the POOLED FUND has at least one of the following characteristics:

a. CLOSED-END
b. FIXED LIFE
c. FIXED COMMITMENT
d. ILLIQUID INVESTMENTS as a significant part of the investment strategy.

1.A.36 The FIRM MUST choose if it will present TIME-WEIGHTED RETURNS, MONEY-WEIGHTED RETURNS, or both for each COMPOSITE or POOLED FUND, and it MUST consistently present the selected returns for each COMPOSITE or POOLED FUND.

1.A.37 If the FIRM chooses to include a GIPS COMPOSITE REPORT or GIPS POOLED FUND REPORT in marketing materials, the FIRM MUST indicate this fact in the marketing materials.

1.A.38 The FIRM MUST notify CFA Institute of its claim of compliance by submitting the GIPS COMPLIANCE NOTIFICATION FORM. This form:

a. MUST be filed when the FIRM initially claims compliance with the GIPS standards.
b. MUST be updated annually with information as of the most recent 31 December, with the exception of FIRM contact information, which MUST be current as of the form submission date.
c. MUST be filed annually thereafter by 30 June.

1.A.39 If the FIRM chooses to be verified, it MUST gain an understanding of the verifier's policies for maintaining independence and MUST consider the verifier's assessment of independence.

## 1.B. Fundamentals of Compliance—Recommendations

1.B.1 The FIRM SHOULD comply with the RECOMMENDATIONS of the GIPS standards, including RECOMMENDATIONS in any Guidance Statements, interpretations, and Q&As published by CFA Institute and the GIPS standards governing bodies.

1.B.2 The FIRM SHOULD update GIPS COMPOSITE REPORTS and GIPS POOLED FUND REPORTS quarterly.

1.B.3 The FIRM SHOULD be verified.

1.B.4 The FIRM SHOULD adopt the broadest, most meaningful definition of the FIRM. The scope of this definition SHOULD include all geographical (country, regional, etc.) offices operating under the same brand name, regardless of the actual name of the individual investment management company.

  

**1.B.5** The FIRM SHOULD provide to each current client, on an annual basis, a GIPS COMPOSITE REPORT of the COMPOSITE in which the client's PORTFOLIO is included.

**1.B.6** The FIRM SHOULD provide to each LIMITED DISTRIBUTION POOLED FUND current investor, on an annual basis, a GIPS POOLED FUND REPORT of the LIMITED DISTRIBUTION POOLED FUND in which the investor is invested.

**1.B.7** If the FIRM is selling participation in a new LIMITED DISTRIBUTION POOLED FUND that does not yet have a track record, the FIRM SHOULD present the most appropriate track record for the new LIMITED DISTRIBUTION POOLED FUND, if available. The most appropriate track record is a GIPS REPORT for a COMPOSITE or another POOLED FUND that is managed according to the same or similar strategy as the new LIMITED DISTRIBUTION POOLED FUND.

# 2. INPUT DATA AND CALCULATION METHODOLOGY

## 2.A. Input Data and Calculation Methodology—Requirements

### Firm Assets, Composite Assets, and Pooled Fund Assets

2.A.1 TOTAL FIRM ASSETS:

a. MUST be the aggregate FAIR VALUE of all discretionary and non-discretionary assets managed by the FIRM. This includes both fee-paying and non-fee-paying PORTFOLIOS.[1]

b. MUST include assets assigned to a SUB-ADVISOR provided the FIRM has discretion over the selection of the SUB-ADVISOR.

c. MUST NOT include ADVISORY-ONLY ASSETS.

d. MUST NOT include uncalled COMMITTED CAPITAL.[2]

2.A.2 TOTAL FIRM ASSETS, COMPOSITE assets, and POOLED FUND assets MUST:

a. Include only actual assets managed by the FIRM.

b. Be calculated net of discretionary leverage and not grossed up as if the leverage did not exist.

2.A.3 The FIRM MUST NOT double count assets when calculating TOTAL FIRM ASSETS, COMPOSITE assets, or POOLED FUND assets.

2.A.4 COMPOSITE and POOLED FUND performance MUST be calculated using only actual assets managed by the FIRM.

### Overlay Exposure

2.A.5 Total FIRM OVERLAY EXPOSURE MUST include all discretionary and non-discretionary OVERLAY STRATEGY PORTFOLIOS for which the FIRM has investment management responsibility.[3]

---

[1] REQUIRED for periods beginning on or after 1 January 2011. For periods prior to 1 January 2011, TOTAL FIRM ASSETS MUST be the aggregate of either the FAIR VALUE or the MARKET VALUE of all discretionary and non-discretionary assets under management within the defined FIRM.

[2] REQUIRED for periods beginning on or after 1 January 2020.

[3] REQUIRED for periods beginning on or after 1 January 2020.

  

2.A.6 When calculating OVERLAY EXPOSURE, the FIRM MUST:[4]

a. Use the notional exposure of the OVERLAY STRATEGY PORTFOLIOS, the value of the underlying PORTFOLIOS being overlaid, or a specified target exposure.

b. Use the same method for all PORTFOLIOS within a COMPOSITE.

2.A.7 When calculating OVERLAY STRATEGY PORTFOLIO returns, the FIRM MUST:[5]

a. Use as the denominator the notional exposure of the OVERLAY STRATEGY PORTFOLIO, the value of the underlying PORTFOLIO being overlaid, or a specified target exposure.

b. Use the same method for all PORTFOLIOS within a COMPOSITE.

## General/Accounting

2.A.8 TOTAL RETURNS MUST be used.

2.A.9 TRADE DATE ACCOUNTING MUST be used.[6]

2.A.10 ACCRUAL ACCOUNTING MUST be used for fixed-income securities and all other investments that earn interest income, except that interest income on cash and cash equivalents may be recognized on a cash basis. Any accrued income MUST be included in the beginning and ending PORTFOLIO values when performance is calculated.

2.A.11 Returns from cash and cash equivalents MUST be included in all return calculations, even if the FIRM does not control the specific cash investment(s).

2.A.12 Returns for periods of less than one year MUST NOT be annualized.

2.A.13 All returns MUST be calculated after the deduction of TRANSACTION COSTS incurred during the period. The FIRM may use estimated TRANSACTION COSTS only for those PORTFOLIOS for which actual TRANSACTION COSTS are not known.

2.A.14 For PORTFOLIOS with BUNDLED FEES, if the FIRM cannot estimate TRANSACTION COSTS or if actual TRANSACTION COSTS cannot be segregated from a BUNDLED FEE:

a. When calculating GROSS-OF-FEES returns, returns MUST be reduced by the entire BUNDLED FEE or the portion of the BUNDLED FEE that includes the TRANSACTION COSTS.

b. When calculating NET-OF-FEES returns, returns MUST be reduced by the entire BUNDLED FEE or the portion of the BUNDLED FEE that includes the TRANSACTION COSTS and the INVESTMENT MANAGEMENT FEE.

2.A.15 All REQUIRED returns MUST be calculated net of discretionary leverage, unless otherwise specified.

---

[4] REQUIRED for periods beginning on or after 1 January 2020.

[5] REQUIRED for periods beginning on or after 1 January 2020.

[6] REQUIRED for periods beginning on or after 1 January 2005.

2.A.16 The FIRM MUST calculate performance in accordance with its COMPOSITE-specific or POOLED FUND–specific calculation policies.

2.A.17 For PORTFOLIOS invested in underlying POOLED FUNDS, all returns MUST reflect the deduction of all fees and expenses charged at the underlying POOLED FUND level, unless the FIRM controls the INVESTMENT MANAGEMENT FEES of the underlying POOLED FUNDS. When the FIRM controls the INVESTMENT MANAGEMENT FEES of the underlying POOLED FUNDS, the FIRM may calculate GROSS-OF-FEES returns that do not reflect the deduction of the underlying POOLED FUND INVESTMENT MANAGEMENT FEES.

2.A.18 When calculating ADDITIONAL RISK MEASURES:

a. The PERIODICITY of the COMPOSITE or POOLED FUND returns and the BENCHMARK returns MUST be the same.

b. The risk measure calculation methodology of the COMPOSITE or POOLED FUND and the BENCHMARK MUST be the same.

## Valuation

2.A.19 PORTFOLIOS MUST be valued in accordance with the definition of FAIR VALUE.[7]

2.A.20 The FIRM MUST value PORTFOLIOS in accordance with the COMPOSITE-specific or POOLED FUND–specific valuation policy.

2.A.21 If the FIRM uses the last available historical price or preliminary, estimated value as FAIR VALUE, the FIRM MUST:

a. Consider it to be the best approximation of the current FAIR VALUE.

b. Assess the difference between the approximation and final value and the effect on COMPOSITE or POOLED FUND assets, TOTAL FIRM ASSETS, and performance, and also make any adjustments when the final value is received.

2.A.22 COMPOSITES and POOLED FUNDS MUST have consistent beginning and ending annual valuation dates. Unless the COMPOSITE or POOLED FUND is reported on a non-calendar fiscal year, the beginning and ending valuation dates MUST be at calendar year end or on the last business day of the year.[8]

[7] REQUIRED for periods beginning on or after 1 January 2011. For periods prior to 1 January 2011, PORTFOLIO valuations (excluding REAL ESTATE and PRIVATE EQUITY) MUST be based on FAIR VALUES or MARKET VALUES. For periods prior to 1 January 2011, REAL ESTATE investments MUST be valued at FAIR VALUE or MARKET VALUE (as previously defined for REAL ESTATE in the 2005 edition of the GIPS standards). For periods ending prior to 1 January 2011, PRIVATE EQUITY investments MUST be valued at FAIR VALUE, according to the GIPS Private Equity Valuation Principles in Appendix D of the 2005 edition of the GIPS standards, or the GIPS Valuation Principles in Chapter II of the 2010 edition of the GIPS standards.

[8] REQUIRED for periods beginning on or after 1 January 2006.

  

## Portfolios—Time-Weighted Returns

2.A.23 When calculating TIME-WEIGHTED RETURNS for PORTFOLIOS that are included in COMPOSITES, all PORTFOLIOS except PRIVATE MARKET INVESTMENT PORTFOLIOS (see 2.A.40) MUST be valued:

a. At least monthly.[9]

b. As of the calendar month end or the last business day of the month.[10]

c. On the date of all LARGE CASH FLOWS. The FIRM MUST define LARGE CASH FLOW for each COMPOSITE to determine when PORTFOLIOS in that COMPOSITE MUST be valued.[11]

2.A.24 When calculating TIME-WEIGHTED RETURNS for all PORTFOLIOS except PRIVATE MARKET INVESTMENT PORTFOLIOS (see 2.A.41) included in COMPOSITES, the FIRM MUST:

a. Calculate returns at least monthly.[12]

b. Calculate monthly returns through the calendar month end or the last business day of the month.[13]

c. Calculate sub-period returns at the time of all LARGE CASH FLOWS, if daily returns are not calculated.[14]

d. For EXTERNAL CASH FLOWS that are not LARGE CASH FLOWS, calculate PORTFOLIO returns that adjust for daily-weighted EXTERNAL CASH FLOWS, if daily returns are not calculated.[15]

e. Treat EXTERNAL CASH FLOWS according to the FIRM'S COMPOSITE-specific policy.

f. Geometrically LINK periodic and sub-period returns.

g. Consistently apply the calculation methodology used for an individual PORTFOLIO.

## Pooled Funds

2.A.25 When calculating TIME-WEIGHTED RETURNS for POOLED FUNDS that are not included in a COMPOSITE, POOLED FUNDS MUST be valued:

a. At least annually.

b. As of the calendar or fiscal year end.

c. Whenever there are subscriptions to or redemptions from the POOLED FUND.

d. As of the period end for any period for which performance is calculated.

---

[9] REQUIRED for periods beginning on or after 1 January 2001. For periods prior to 1 January 2001, PORTFOLIOS MUST be valued at least quarterly.

[10] REQUIRED for periods beginning on or after 1 January 2010.

[11] REQUIRED for periods beginning on or after 1 January 2010.

[12] REQUIRED for periods beginning on or after 1 January 2001.

[13] REQUIRED for periods beginning on or after 1 January 2010.

[14] REQUIRED for periods beginning on or after 1 January 2010.

[15] REQUIRED for periods beginning on or after 1 January 2005.

2.A.26 When calculating TIME-WEIGHTED RETURNS for POOLED FUNDS that are not included in a COMPOSITE, the FIRM MUST:

a. Calculate returns at least annually.

b. Calculate annual returns through the calendar or fiscal year end or the last business day of the year.

c. Calculate sub-period returns at the time of all subscriptions and redemptions.

d. Geometrically LINK periodic and sub-period returns.

e. When calculating POOLED FUND NET RETURNS, calculate POOLED FUND NET RETURNS that are net of TOTAL POOLED FUND FEES.

2.A.27 The FIRM MUST establish a POOLED FUND INCEPTION DATE for each POOLED FUND to determine when the POOLED FUND'S track record begins.[16]

## Money-Weighted Returns

2.A.28 When calculating MONEY-WEIGHTED RETURNS, the FIRM MUST value PORTFOLIOS at least annually and as of the period end for any period for which performance is calculated.

2.A.29 When calculating MONEY-WEIGHTED RETURNS, the FIRM MUST:

a. Calculate annualized SINCE-INCEPTION MONEY-WEIGHTED RETURNS.

b. Calculate MONEY-WEIGHTED RETURNS using daily EXTERNAL CASH FLOWS.[17]

c. Include stock DISTRIBUTIONS as EXTERNAL CASH FLOWS and value stock DISTRIBUTIONS at the time of DISTRIBUTION.

d. When calculating POOLED FUND NET RETURNS, calculate POOLED FUND NET RETURNS that are net of TOTAL POOLED FUND FEES.

## Net Returns

2.A.30 When calculating COMPOSITE NET-OF-FEES returns, INVESTMENT MANAGEMENT FEES used in the calculation MUST be either:

a. Actual INVESTMENT MANAGEMENT FEES incurred by each PORTFOLIO in the COMPOSITE, or

b. A model INVESTMENT MANAGEMENT FEE appropriate to PROSPECTIVE CLIENTS.

---

[16] REQUIRED for periods beginning on or after 1 January 2020. For periods prior to 1 January 2020, PRIVATE EQUITY PRIMARY FUNDS MUST be included in at least one COMPOSITE defined by VINTAGE YEAR and investment mandate, objective, or strategy. For periods prior to 1 January 2020, PRIVATE EQUITY POOLED FUNDS OF FUNDS MUST be included in at least one COMPOSITE defined by VINTAGE YEAR of the POOLED FUND OF FUNDS and/or investment mandate, objective, or strategy.

[17] Daily EXTERNAL CASH FLOWS are REQUIRED beginning 1 January 2020. Prior to 1 January 2020, quarterly or more frequent EXTERNAL CASH FLOWS MUST be used.

  

**2.A.31** If the FIRM uses model INVESTMENT MANAGEMENT FEES to calculate COMPOSITE NET-OF-FEES returns, the returns calculated MUST be equal to or lower than those that would have been calculated using actual INVESTMENT MANAGEMENT FEES.

**2.A.32** When calculating POOLED FUND NET RETURNS, TOTAL POOLED FUND FEES used in the calculation MUST be either:

a. Actual TOTAL POOLED FUND FEES, or

b. A model TOTAL POOLED FUND FEE appropriate to PROSPECTIVE INVESTORS.

**2.A.33** If the FIRM uses model TOTAL POOLED FUND FEES to calculate POOLED FUND NET RETURNS, the returns calculated MUST be equal to or lower than those that would have been calculated using actual TOTAL POOLED FUND FEES.

**2.A.34** When calculating COMPOSITE NET-OF-FEES returns and POOLED FUND NET RETURNS, the FIRM MUST reflect any PERFORMANCE-BASED FEE CLAWBACK in the period in which it is repaid.[18]

## Composite Returns

**2.A.35** COMPOSITE TIME-WEIGHTED RETURNS except PRIVATE MARKET INVESTMENT COMPOSITES (see 2.A.42) MUST be calculated at least monthly.[19]

**2.A.36** COMPOSITE TIME-WEIGHTED RETURNS MUST be calculated by using one of the following approaches:

a. Asset-weighting the individual PORTFOLIO returns using beginning-of-period values;

b. Asset-weighting the individual PORTFOLIO returns using a method that reflects both beginning-of-period values and EXTERNAL CASH FLOWS; or

c. Using the aggregate method.

**2.A.37** COMPOSITE GROSS-OF-FEES returns MUST reflect the deduction of TRANSACTION COSTS.

**2.A.38** COMPOSITE NET-OF-FEES returns MUST reflect the deduction of TRANSACTION COSTS and INVESTMENT MANAGEMENT FEES.

**2.A.39** When calculating COMPOSITE MONEY-WEIGHTED RETURNS, the FIRM MUST calculate COMPOSITE returns by aggregating the PORTFOLIO-level information for those PORTFOLIOS included in the COMPOSITE.

[18] REQUIRED for periods beginning on or after 1 January 2020.

[19] REQUIRED for periods beginning on or after 1 January 2010. For periods beginning on or after 1 January 2006 and ending prior to 1 January 2010, COMPOSITE returns MUST be calculated at least quarterly.

## Private Market Investments

2.A.40 When calculating TIME-WEIGHTED RETURNS for PRIVATE MARKET INVESTMENT PORTFOLIOS that are included in COMPOSITES, PRIVATE MARKET INVESTMENT PORTFOLIOS MUST be valued:

a. At least quarterly.[20]

b. As of each quarter end or the last business day of the quarter.[21]

2.A.41 When calculating TIME-WEIGHTED RETURNS for PRIVATE MARKET INVESTMENT PORTFOLIOS that are included in COMPOSITES, the FIRM MUST:

a. Calculate returns at least quarterly.[22]

b. Calculate quarterly returns through the calendar quarter end or the last business day of the quarter.[23]

c. Calculate PORTFOLIO returns that adjust for daily-weighted EXTERNAL CASH FLOWS.[24]

d. Treat EXTERNAL CASH FLOWS according to the FIRM'S COMPOSITE-specific policy.

e. Geometrically LINK periodic and sub-period returns.

f. Consistently apply the calculation methodology used for an individual PORTFOLIO.

2.A.42 COMPOSITE TIME-WEIGHTED RETURNS for PRIVATE MARKET INVESTMENT COMPOSITES MUST be calculated at least quarterly.

## Real Estate

2.A.43 REAL ESTATE investments in a REAL ESTATE OPEN-END FUND MUST have an EXTERNAL VALUATION at least once every 12 months.[25]

2.A.44 REAL ESTATE investments that are not in a REAL ESTATE OPEN-END FUND MUST:[26]

a. Have an EXTERNAL VALUATION at least once every 12 months unless client agreements stipulate otherwise, in which case REAL ESTATE investments MUST have an EXTERNAL VALUATION at least once every 36 months or per the client agreement if

---

[20] REQUIRED for periods beginning on or after 1 January 2008.

[21] REQUIRED for periods beginning on or after 1 January 2010.

[22] REQUIRED for periods beginning on or after 1 January 2008.

[23] REQUIRED for periods beginning on or after 1 January 2010.

[24] REQUIRED for periods beginning on or after 1 January 2010.

[25] REQUIRED for periods beginning on or after 1 January 2020. For periods beginning on or after 1 January 2012 and ending prior to 1 January 2020, REAL ESTATE investments MUST have an EXTERNAL VALUATION at least once every 12 months unless client agreements stipulate otherwise, in which case REAL ESTATE investments MUST have an EXTERNAL VALUATION at least once every 36 months or per the client agreement if the client agreement REQUIRES EXTERNAL VALUATIONS more frequently than every 36 months. For periods beginning on or after 1 January 2006 and ending prior to 1 January 2012, REAL ESTATE investments MUST have an EXTERNAL VALUATION at least once every 36 months.

[26] REQUIRED for periods beginning on or after 1 January 2012. For periods beginning on or after 1 January 2006 and ending prior to 1 January 2012, REAL ESTATE investments MUST have an EXTERNAL VALUATION at least once every 36 months or be subject to an annual financial statement audit performed by an independent public accounting firm.

  

the client agreement REQUIRES EXTERNAL VALUATIONS more frequently than every 36 months; or

b. Be subject to an annual financial statement audit performed by an independent public accounting firm. The REAL ESTATE investments MUST be accounted for at FAIR VALUE, and the most recent audited financial statements available MUST contain an unmodified opinion issued by an independent public accounting firm.

2.A.45 EXTERNAL VALUATIONS for REAL ESTATE investments MUST be performed by an independent third party who is a professionally designated or certified commercial property valuer or appraiser. In markets where these professionals are not available, the FIRM MUST take necessary steps to ensure that only qualified independent property valuers or appraisers are used.

2.A.46 The FIRM MUST NOT use EXTERNAL VALUATIONS for REAL ESTATE investments when the valuer's or appraiser's fee is contingent upon the investment's appraised value.

## Carve-Outs

2.A.47 When calculating NET-OF-FEES returns of COMPOSITES containing CARVE-OUTS, the INVESTMENT MANAGEMENT FEES for the CARVE-OUTS MUST be representative of the INVESTMENT MANAGEMENT FEES charged or that would be charged to the PROSPECTIVE CLIENT:

a. When presenting performance to a PROSPECTIVE CLIENT for a standalone PORTFOLIO, the INVESTMENT MANAGEMENT FEE MUST be representative of the INVESTMENT MANAGEMENT FEES for a standalone PORTFOLIO managed according to that strategy.

b. When presenting performance to a PROSPECTIVE CLIENT for a multi-asset strategy PORTFOLIO, the INVESTMENT MANAGEMENT FEE MUST be representative of the INVESTMENT MANAGEMENT FEES for a multi-asset strategy PORTFOLIO managed according to that strategy.

## Wrap Fee

2.A.48 When calculating returns to be presented to a WRAP FEE PROSPECTIVE CLIENT, returns MUST be calculated net of the entire WRAP FEE. This is applicable to all WRAP FEE PORTFOLIOS in the COMPOSITE as well as any non–WRAP FEE PORTFOLIOS in the COMPOSITE.

### Side Pockets and Subscription Lines of Credit

2.A.49 All COMPOSITE and POOLED FUND returns MUST include the effect of any discretionary SIDE POCKETS held by PORTFOLIOS in the COMPOSITE or the POOLED FUND.[27]

2.A.50 When calculating MONEY-WEIGHTED RETURNS for COMPOSITES and POOLED FUNDS without the SUBSCRIPTION LINES OF CREDIT, the FIRM MUST include the cash flows from the SUBSCRIPTION LINES OF CREDIT.[28]

## 2.B. Input Data and Calculation Methodology—Recommendations

2.B.1 The FIRM SHOULD value PORTFOLIOS on the date of all EXTERNAL CASH FLOWS.

2.B.2 Valuations SHOULD be obtained from a qualified independent third party.

2.B.3 ACCRUAL ACCOUNTING SHOULD be used for dividends (as of the ex-dividend date).

2.B.4 The FIRM SHOULD accrue INVESTMENT MANAGEMENT FEES.

2.B.5 Returns SHOULD be calculated net of non-reclaimable withholding taxes on dividends, interest, and capital gains. Reclaimable withholding taxes SHOULD be accrued.

2.B.6 The FIRM SHOULD incorporate the following hierarchy into its policies and procedures for determining FAIR VALUE for PORTFOLIO investments on a COMPOSITE-specific or POOLED FUND–specific basis.

- a. Investments MUST be valued using objective, observable, unadjusted quoted market prices for identical investments in active markets on the measurement date, if available. If such prices are not available, then investments SHOULD be valued using;
- b. Objective, observable quoted market prices for similar investments in active markets. If such prices are not available or appropriate, then investments SHOULD be valued using;
- c. Quoted prices for identical or similar investments in markets that are not active (markets in which there are few transactions for the investment, the prices are not current, or price quotations vary substantially over time and/or between market makers). If such prices are not available or appropriate, then investments SHOULD be valued based on;
- d. Market-based inputs, other than quoted prices, that are observable for the investment. If such inputs are not available or appropriate, then investments SHOULD be valued based on;

[27] REQUIRED for periods beginning on or after 1 October 2012.

[28] REQUIRED for MONEY-WEIGHTED RETURNS for periods ending on or after 31 December 2020.

  

e. Subjective, unobservable inputs for the investment where markets are not active at the measurement date. Unobservable inputs SHOULD be used to measure FAIR VALUE only when observable inputs and prices are not available or appropriate. Unobservable inputs reflect the FIRM's own assumptions about the assumptions that market participants would use in pricing the investment and SHOULD be developed based on the best information available under the circumstances.

**2.B.7** The FIRM SHOULD use GROSS-OF-FEES returns when calculating risk measures.

**2.B.8** PRIVATE MARKET INVESTMENTS SHOULD have an EXTERNAL VALUATION at least once every 12 months.

  

# 3. COMPOSITE AND POOLED FUND MAINTENANCE

## 3.A. Composite and Pooled Fund Maintenance—Requirements

3.A.1 The FIRM MUST create COMPOSITES for the FIRM's strategies that are managed for or offered as a SEGREGATED ACCOUNT.

3.A.2 All actual, fee-paying, discretionary SEGREGATED ACCOUNTS MUST be included in at least one COMPOSITE. Non-discretionary PORTFOLIOS MUST NOT be included in COMPOSITES.

3.A.3 All actual, fee-paying, discretionary POOLED FUNDS MUST be included in at least one COMPOSITE if they meet a COMPOSITE DEFINITION. The FIRM is not REQUIRED to create a COMPOSITE that only includes one or more POOLED FUNDS unless the FIRM offers the strategy as a SEGREGATED ACCOUNT. The FIRM may terminate any COMPOSITE that was created solely to include one or more POOLED FUNDS if the COMPOSITE is not representative of the FIRM's strategy offered as a SEGREGATED ACCOUNT.

3.A.4 Non-fee-paying discretionary PORTFOLIOS may be included in a COMPOSITE. If the FIRM includes non-fee-paying discretionary PORTFOLIOS in a COMPOSITE, those PORTFOLIOS MUST be subject to the same policies and procedures as fee-paying PORTFOLIOS.

3.A.5 COMPOSITES MUST be defined according to investment mandate, objective, or strategy. COMPOSITES MUST include all PORTFOLIOS, including SEGREGATED ACCOUNTS and POOLED FUNDS, that meet the COMPOSITE DEFINITION. The FIRM MUST NOT exclude PORTFOLIOS from COMPOSITES based solely on legal structure differences.

3.A.6 Any change to a COMPOSITE DEFINITION MUST NOT be applied retroactively.

3.A.7 COMPOSITES MUST include new PORTFOLIOS on a timely and consistent COMPOSITE-specific basis after each PORTFOLIO comes under management.

3.A.8 COMPOSITES MUST include only those PORTFOLIOS that are managed for the full performance measurement period for which the COMPOSITE return is calculated. PORTFOLIOS that are not managed for the full performance measurement period MUST NOT be included in the COMPOSITE.

3.A.9 Terminated PORTFOLIOS MUST be included in the historical performance of the COMPOSITE up to the last full measurement period that each PORTFOLIO was under management and for which the FIRM has discretion.

3.A.10 PORTFOLIOS MUST NOT be moved from one COMPOSITE to another unless documented client-directed changes to a PORTFOLIO's investment mandate, objective, or strategy or the redefinition of the COMPOSITE make it appropriate. The historical performance of the PORTFOLIO MUST remain with the original COMPOSITE. PORTFOLIOS MUST NOT be moved into or out of COMPOSITES as a result of the FIRM's tactical changes.

**3.A.11** If the FIRM sets a minimum asset level for PORTFOLIOS to be included in a COMPOSITE, the FIRM:

a. MUST NOT include PORTFOLIOS below the COMPOSITE-specific minimum asset level in that COMPOSITE.

b. MUST NOT apply retroactively any changes to that COMPOSITE-specific minimum asset level.

**3.A.12** A FIRM that removes PORTFOLIOS from COMPOSITES because of SIGNIFICANT CASH FLOWS MUST define "significant" on an EX ANTE, COMPOSITE-specific basis and MUST consistently follow the COMPOSITE-specific policy.

**3.A.13** A FIRM that uses TEMPORARY NEW ACCOUNTS to remove the effect of a SIGNIFICANT CASH FLOW MUST establish policies on an EX ANTE, COMPOSITE-specific basis. TEMPORARY NEW ACCOUNTS MUST NOT be included in COMPOSITE performance.

## Wrap Fee

**3.A.14** The FIRM MUST include the performance record of actual WRAP FEE PORTFOLIOS in appropriate COMPOSITES in accordance with the FIRM's established PORTFOLIO inclusion policies. Once established, these COMPOSITES (containing actual WRAP FEE PORTFOLIOS) MUST be used when presenting GIPS COMPOSITE REPORTS to WRAP FEE PROSPECTIVE CLIENTS.

## Carve-Outs

**3.A.15** Any CARVE-OUT included in a COMPOSITE MUST include cash and any related income. Cash may be:

a. Accounted for separately, or

b. Allocated synthetically to the CARVE-OUT on a timely and consistent basis.

**3.A.16** Any CARVE-OUT included in a COMPOSITE MUST be representative of a standalone PORTFOLIO managed or intended to be managed according to that strategy.

**3.A.17** When the FIRM creates a CARVE-OUT of a particular strategy, allocates cash to the CARVE-OUT, and includes the CARVE-OUT in a COMPOSITE, the FIRM MUST create CARVE-OUTS with allocated cash from all PORTFOLIOS and PORTFOLIO segments within the FIRM managed to that strategy and MUST include those CARVE-OUTS with allocated cash in the COMPOSITE.

  

3.A.18 When the FIRM has or obtains standalone PORTFOLIOS managed in the same strategy as the CARVE-OUTS with allocated cash, the FIRM MUST create a separate COMPOSITE for the standalone PORTFOLIOS.

3.A.19 The FIRM MUST NOT combine different COMPOSITES, POOLED FUNDS, or CARVE-OUTS to create a simulated strategy and present it as a COMPOSITE.

## 3.B. Composite and Pooled Fund Maintenance—Recommendations

3.B.1 If the FIRM sets a minimum asset level for PORTFOLIOS to be included in a COMPOSITE, the FIRM SHOULD NOT present a GIPS COMPOSITE REPORT to a PROSPECTIVE CLIENT known not to meet the COMPOSITE's minimum asset level.

3.B.2 To remove the effect of a SIGNIFICANT CASH FLOW, the FIRM SHOULD use a TEMPORARY NEW ACCOUNT.

  

# 4. COMPOSITE TIME-WEIGHTED RETURN REPORT

**The following provisions apply to COMPOSITES that include TIME-WEIGHTED RETURNS in a GIPS COMPOSITE REPORT.**

## 4.A. Presentation and Reporting—Requirements

4.A.1 The FIRM MUST present in each GIPS COMPOSITE REPORT:

a. At least five years of performance (or for the period since the COMPOSITE INCEPTION DATE if the COMPOSITE has been in existence less than five years) that meets the REQUIREMENTS of the GIPS standards. After the FIRM presents a minimum of five years of GIPS-compliant performance (or for the period since the COMPOSITE INCEPTION DATE if the COMPOSITE has been in existence less than five years), the FIRM MUST present an additional year of performance each year, building up to a minimum of 10 years of GIPS-compliant performance.

b. COMPOSITE returns for each annual period.

c. When the initial period is less than a full year, the return from the COMPOSITE INCEPTION DATE through the initial annual period end.[29]

d. When the COMPOSITE terminates, the return from the last annual period end through the COMPOSITE TERMINATION DATE.[30]

e. The TOTAL RETURN for the BENCHMARK for each annual period and for all other periods for which COMPOSITE returns are presented, unless the FIRM determines there is no appropriate BENCHMARK.

f. The number of PORTFOLIOS in the COMPOSITE as of each annual period end. If the COMPOSITE contains five or fewer PORTFOLIOS at period end, the number of PORTFOLIOS is not REQUIRED.

g. COMPOSITE assets as of each annual period end.

h. TOTAL FIRM ASSETS as of each annual period end.[31]

i. A measure of INTERNAL DISPERSION of individual PORTFOLIO annual returns for each annual period. If the COMPOSITE contains five or fewer PORTFOLIOS for the full year, a measure of INTERNAL DISPERSION is not REQUIRED.

[29] REQUIRED for COMPOSITES with a COMPOSITE INCEPTION DATE of 1 January 2011 or later.

[30] REQUIRED for COMPOSITES with a COMPOSITE TERMINATION DATE of 1 January 2011 or later.

[31] REQUIRED for periods ending on or after 31 December 2020. For periods ending prior to 31 December 2020, the FIRM may present either TOTAL FIRM ASSETS or COMPOSITE assets as a percentage of TOTAL FIRM ASSETS.

  

j. For COMPOSITES for which monthly COMPOSITE returns are available, the three-year annualized EX POST STANDARD DEVIATION (using monthly returns) of the COMPOSITE and the BENCHMARK as of each annual period end.[32]

4.A.2 The FIRM MUST present the percentage of the total FAIR VALUE of COMPOSITE assets that were valued using subjective unobservable inputs (as described in provision 2.B.6.e) as of the most recent annual period end, if such investments represent a material amount of COMPOSITE assets.

4.A.3 The FIRM MUST clearly label or identify:

a. The periods that are presented.

b. If COMPOSITE returns are GROSS-OF-FEES or NET-OF-FEES.

4.A.4 If the FIRM includes more than one BENCHMARK in the GIPS COMPOSITE REPORT, the FIRM MUST present and disclose all REQUIRED information for all BENCHMARKS presented.

4.A.5 If the COMPOSITE loses all of its member PORTFOLIOS, the COMPOSITE track record MUST end. If PORTFOLIOS are later added to the COMPOSITE, the COMPOSITE track record MUST restart. The periods both before and after the break in track record MUST be presented, with the break in performance clearly shown. The FIRM MUST NOT LINK performance prior to the break in track record to the performance after the break in track record.

4.A.6 If the COMPOSITE includes CARVE-OUTS with allocated cash, the FIRM MUST present the percentage of COMPOSITE assets represented by CARVE-OUTS with allocated cash as of each annual period end.

4.A.7 If the COMPOSITE includes non-fee-paying PORTFOLIOS, the FIRM MUST present the percentage of COMPOSITE assets represented by non-fee-paying PORTFOLIOS as of each annual period end when NET-OF-FEES returns are presented and are calculated using actual INVESTMENT MANAGEMENT FEES.

4.A.8 If the FIRM chooses to present COMPOSITE uncalled COMMITTED CAPITAL or a combination of COMPOSITE assets and COMPOSITE uncalled COMMITTED CAPITAL, the FIRM MUST:

a. Present COMPOSITE uncalled COMMITTED CAPITAL for the same periods for which the combination of COMPOSITE assets and COMPOSITE uncalled COMMITTED CAPITAL is presented.

b. Clearly label COMPOSITE uncalled COMMITTED CAPITAL as such.

c. Clearly label the combination of COMPOSITE assets and COMPOSITE uncalled COMMITTED CAPITAL as such.

[32] REQUIRED for periods ending on or after 1 January 2011.

  

**4.A.9** If the FIRM chooses to present FIRM-wide uncalled COMMITTED CAPITAL or a combination of TOTAL FIRM ASSETS and FIRM-wide uncalled COMMITTED CAPITAL, the FIRM MUST:

a. Present FIRM-wide uncalled COMMITTED CAPITAL for the same periods for which the combination of TOTAL FIRM ASSETS and FIRM-wide uncalled COMMITTED CAPITAL is presented.

b. Clearly label FIRM-wide uncalled COMMITTED CAPITAL as such.

c. Clearly label the combination of TOTAL FIRM ASSETS and FIRM-wide uncalled COMMITTED CAPITAL as such.

**4.A.10** If the FIRM chooses to present ADVISORY-ONLY ASSETS that reflect the COMPOSITE'S investment mandate, objective, or strategy, or a combination of COMPOSITE assets and ADVISORY-ONLY ASSETS that reflect the COMPOSITE'S investment mandate, objective, or strategy, the FIRM MUST:

a. Present ADVISORY-ONLY ASSETS that reflect the COMPOSITE'S investment mandate, objective, or strategy for the same periods for which the combination of COMPOSITE assets and ADVISORY-ONLY ASSETS that reflect the COMPOSITE'S investment mandate, objective, or strategy is presented.

b. Clearly label ADVISORY-ONLY ASSETS that reflect the COMPOSITE'S investment mandate, objective, or strategy as such.

c. Clearly label the combination of COMPOSITE assets and ADVISORY-ONLY ASSETS that reflect the COMPOSITE'S investment mandate, objective, or strategy as such.

**4.A.11** If the FIRM chooses to present FIRM-wide ADVISORY-ONLY ASSETS or a combination of TOTAL FIRM ASSETS and FIRM-wide ADVISORY-ONLY ASSETS, the FIRM MUST:

a. Present FIRM-wide ADVISORY-ONLY ASSETS for the same periods for which the combination of TOTAL FIRM ASSETS and FIRM-wide ADVISORY-ONLY ASSETS is presented.

b. Clearly label FIRM-wide ADVISORY-ONLY ASSETS as such.

c. Clearly label the combination of TOTAL FIRM ASSETS and FIRM-wide ADVISORY-ONLY ASSETS as such.

**4.A.12** All REQUIRED and RECOMMENDED information in the GIPS COMPOSITE REPORT MUST be presented in the same currency.

**4.A.13** When the FIRM presents the performance of a COMPOSITE that includes CARVE-OUTS with allocated cash and also has a COMPOSITE of standalone PORTFOLIOS managed according to the same strategy, the FIRM MUST present for the COMPOSITE of standalone PORTFOLIOS:

a. The COMPOSITE returns for each annual period for which the COMPOSITE of standalone PORTFOLIOS exists, and

b. The COMPOSITE assets as of each annual period end for which the COMPOSITE of standalone PORTFOLIOS exists.

  

This information MUST be included in the GIPS COMPOSITE REPORT of the COMPOSITE that includes CARVE-OUTS with allocated cash.

4.A.14 For OVERLAY STRATEGY COMPOSITES, the FIRM MUST present COMPOSITE OVERLAY EXPOSURE as of each annual period end. For those periods for which the FIRM presents COMPOSITE OVERLAY EXPOSURE, the FIRM may choose not to present COMPOSITE assets.[33]

4.A.15 For OVERLAY STRATEGY COMPOSITES, the FIRM is not REQUIRED to present TOTAL FIRM ASSETS and may instead choose to present total FIRM OVERLAY EXPOSURE as of each annual period end.

4.A.16 For WRAP FEE COMPOSITES, when the FIRM presents performance to a WRAP FEE PROSPECTIVE CLIENT, the FIRM MUST present:

a. The COMPOSITE that includes the performance of all actual WRAP FEE PORTFOLIOS, if any, managed according to the COMPOSITE investment mandate, objective, or strategy, regardless of the WRAP FEE sponsor.

b. COMPOSITE performance that is net of the entire WRAP FEE.

c. The percentage of COMPOSITE assets represented by WRAP FEE PORTFOLIOS as of each annual period end.

4.A.17 For WRAP FEE COMPOSITES, when the FIRM presents PURE GROSS-OF-FEES returns, the FIRM MUST:

a. Clearly label returns as PURE GROSS-OF-FEES.

b. Identify PURE GROSS-OF-FEES returns as SUPPLEMENTAL INFORMATION.

4.A.18 Any SUPPLEMENTAL INFORMATION included in the GIPS COMPOSITE REPORT:

a. MUST relate directly to the COMPOSITE.

b. MUST NOT contradict or conflict with the REQUIRED or RECOMMENDED information in the GIPS COMPOSITE REPORT.

c. MUST be clearly labeled as SUPPLEMENTAL INFORMATION.

## 4.B. Presentation and Reporting—Recommendations

4.B.1 The FIRM SHOULD present both GROSS-OF-FEES and NET-OF-FEES COMPOSITE returns.

4.B.2 The FIRM SHOULD present the following items:

a. Cumulative returns of the COMPOSITE and the BENCHMARK for all periods.

b. Equal-weighted COMPOSITE returns.

c. Quarterly and/or monthly returns.

d. Annualized COMPOSITE and BENCHMARK returns for periods longer than 12 months.

[33] REQUIRED for periods ending on or after 31 December 2020.

  

4.B.3 For all periods for which an annualized EX POST STANDARD DEVIATION of the COMPOSITE and the BENCHMARK are presented, the FIRM SHOULD present the corresponding annualized return of the COMPOSITE and the BENCHMARK.

4.B.4 For all periods greater than three years for which an annualized return of the COMPOSITE and the BENCHMARK are presented, the FIRM SHOULD present the corresponding annualized EX POST STANDARD DEVIATION (using monthly returns) of the COMPOSITE and the BENCHMARK.

4.B.5 The FIRM SHOULD present relevant EX POST ADDITIONAL RISK MEASURES for the COMPOSITE and the BENCHMARK.

4.B.6 The FIRM SHOULD present more than 10 years of annual performance in the GIPS COMPOSITE REPORT.

4.B.7 The FIRM SHOULD present PROPRIETARY ASSETS as a percentage of COMPOSITE assets as of each annual period end.

4.B.8 If the FIRM uses preliminary, estimated values as FAIR VALUE, the FIRM SHOULD present the percentage of assets in the COMPOSITE that were valued using preliminary, estimated values as of each annual period end.

4.B.9 For REAL ESTATE COMPOSITES, the FIRM SHOULD present COMPOSITE and BENCHMARK COMPONENT RETURNS for all periods presented.

4.B.10 If the FIRM has COMMITTED CAPITAL, the FIRM SHOULD present FIRM-wide uncalled COMMITTED CAPITAL as of each annual period end.

## 4.C. Disclosure—Requirements

4.C.1 Once the FIRM has met all the applicable REQUIREMENTS of the GIPS standards, the FIRM MUST disclose its compliance with the GIPS standards using one of the following compliance statements. The compliance statement for a COMPOSITE MUST only be used in a GIPS COMPOSITE REPORT.

a. For a FIRM that is verified:

"[Insert name of FIRM] claims compliance with the Global Investment Performance Standards (GIPS®) and has prepared and presented this report in compliance with the GIPS standards. [Insert name of FIRM] has been independently verified for the periods [insert dates]. The verification report(s) is/are available upon request.

"A firm that claims compliance with the GIPS standards must establish policies and procedures for complying with all the applicable requirements of the GIPS standards. Verification provides assurance on whether the firm's policies and procedures related to composite and pooled fund maintenance, as well as the calculation, presentation, and distribution of performance, have been designed in compliance with the GIPS standards and have been implemented on a firm-wide basis. Verification does not provide assurance on the accuracy of any specific performance report."

b. For COMPOSITES of a verified FIRM that have also had a PERFORMANCE EXAMINATION:

"[Insert name of FIRM] claims compliance with the Global Investment Performance Standards (GIPS®) and has prepared and presented this report in compliance with the GIPS standards. [Insert name of FIRM] has been independently verified for the periods [insert dates].

"A firm that claims compliance with the GIPS standards must establish policies and procedures for complying with all the applicable requirements of the GIPS standards. Verification provides assurance on whether the firm's policies and procedures related to composite and pooled fund maintenance, as well as the calculation, presentation, and distribution of performance, have been designed in compliance with the GIPS standards and have been implemented on a firm-wide basis. The [insert name of COMPOSITE] has had a performance examination for the periods [insert dates]. The verification and performance examination reports are available upon request."

The compliance statement for a FIRM that is verified or for COMPOSITES of a verified FIRM that have also had a PERFORMANCE EXAMINATION is complete only when both paragraphs are shown together, one after the other.

c. For a FIRM that has not been verified:

"[Insert name of FIRM] claims compliance with the Global Investment Performance Standards (GIPS®) and has prepared and presented this report in compliance with the GIPS standards. [Insert name of FIRM] has not been independently verified."

The FIRM MUST NOT exclude any portion of the respective compliance statement. Any modifications to the compliance statement MUST be additive.

4.C.2 The FIRM MUST disclose the following: "GIPS® is a registered trademark of CFA Institute. CFA Institute does not endorse or promote this organization, nor does it warrant the accuracy or quality of the content contained herein."

4.C.3 The FIRM MUST disclose the definition of the FIRM used to determine TOTAL FIRM ASSETS and FIRM-wide compliance.

4.C.4 The FIRM MUST disclose the COMPOSITE DESCRIPTION.

  

**4.C.5** The FIRM MUST disclose:

- **a.** The BENCHMARK DESCRIPTION, which MUST include the key features of the BENCHMARK or the name of the BENCHMARK for a readily recognized index or other point of reference.
- **b.** The PERIODICITY of the BENCHMARK if BENCHMARK returns are calculated less frequently than monthly.

**4.C.6** When presenting GROSS-OF-FEES returns, the FIRM MUST disclose if any other fees are deducted in addition to TRANSACTION COSTS.

**4.C.7** When presenting NET-OF-FEES returns, the FIRM MUST disclose:

- **a.** If any other fees are deducted in addition to INVESTMENT MANAGEMENT FEES and TRANSACTION COSTS.
- **b.** If NET-OF-FEES returns are net of any PERFORMANCE-BASED FEES or CARRIED INTEREST.
- **c.** If model or actual INVESTMENT MANAGEMENT FEES are used.
- **d.** If model INVESTMENT MANAGEMENT FEES are used, and COMPOSITE GROSS-OF-FEES returns are not presented, the model INVESTMENT MANAGEMENT FEE used to calculate NET-OF-FEES returns.[34]
- **e.** If model INVESTMENT MANAGEMENT FEES are used, the methodology used to calculate NET-OF-FEES returns.

**4.C.8** The FIRM MUST disclose which fees and expenses other than INVESTMENT MANAGEMENT FEES (e.g., research costs) are separately charged by the FIRM to clients, if material.

**4.C.9** The FIRM MUST disclose or otherwise indicate the reporting currency.

**4.C.10** The FIRM MUST disclose which measure of INTERNAL DISPERSION is presented.

**4.C.11** The FIRM MUST disclose the current FEE SCHEDULE appropriate to PROSPECTIVE CLIENTS or PROSPECTIVE INVESTORS.

- **a.** When presenting performance to a PROSPECTIVE CLIENT for a standalone PORTFOLIO, the FEE SCHEDULE MUST reflect the FEE SCHEDULE for a standalone PORTFOLIO managed according to that strategy.
- **b.** When presenting performance of a COMPOSITE that includes CARVE-OUTS to a PROSPECTIVE CLIENT for a multi-asset strategy PORTFOLIO, the FEE SCHEDULE MUST reflect the FEE SCHEDULE for a multi-asset strategy PORTFOLIO managed according to that strategy.
- **c.** When presenting a WRAP FEE COMPOSITE to a WRAP FEE PROSPECTIVE CLIENT, the FEE SCHEDULE MUST reflect the total WRAP FEE.
- **d.** When presenting a GIPS COMPOSITE REPORT to a PROSPECTIVE INVESTOR for a POOLED FUND included in the COMPOSITE, the FIRM MUST disclose the POOLED FUND'S current FEE SCHEDULE and EXPENSE RATIO.

---

[34] REQUIRED for periods ending on or after 31 December 2020.

**4.C.12** If the FEE SCHEDULE includes PERFORMANCE-BASED FEES or CARRIED INTEREST, the FIRM MUST disclose the PERFORMANCE-BASED FEE DESCRIPTION or CARRIED INTEREST DESCRIPTION.

**4.C.13** The FIRM MUST disclose the COMPOSITE INCEPTION DATE.

**4.C.14** The FIRM MUST disclose the COMPOSITE CREATION DATE.

**4.C.15** The FIRM MUST disclose that the following lists are available upon request, if applicable:

a. List of COMPOSITE DESCRIPTIONS.

b. List of POOLED FUND DESCRIPTIONS for LIMITED DISTRIBUTION POOLED FUNDS.

c. List of BROAD DISTRIBUTION POOLED FUNDS.

**4.C.16** The FIRM MUST disclose that policies for valuing investments, calculating performance, and preparing GIPS REPORTS are available upon request.

**4.C.17** The FIRM MUST disclose how leverage, derivatives, and short positions have been used historically, if material.

**4.C.18** If estimated TRANSACTION COSTS are used, the FIRM MUST disclose:

a. That estimated TRANSACTION COSTS were used.

b. The estimated TRANSACTION COSTS used and how they were determined.

**4.C.19** The FIRM MUST disclose all significant events that would help a PROSPECTIVE CLIENT interpret the GIPS COMPOSITE REPORT. This disclosure MUST be included for a minimum of one year and for as long as it is relevant to interpreting the track record.

**4.C.20** For any performance presented for periods prior to the MINIMUM EFFECTIVE COMPLIANCE DATE that does not comply with the GIPS standards, the FIRM MUST disclose the periods of non-compliance.

**4.C.21** If the FIRM is redefined, the FIRM MUST disclose the date and description of the redefinition.

**4.C.22** If the COMPOSITE is redefined, the FIRM MUST disclose the date and description of the redefinition.

**4.C.23** The FIRM MUST disclose changes to the name of the COMPOSITE. This disclosure MUST be included for a minimum of one year and for as long as it is relevant to interpreting the track record.

**4.C.24** The FIRM MUST disclose:

a. The minimum asset level, if any, below which PORTFOLIOS are not included in the COMPOSITE.

b. Any changes to the minimum asset level.

**4.C.25** The FIRM MUST disclose if COMPOSITE returns are gross or net of withholding taxes, if material.

**4.C.26** The FIRM MUST disclose if BENCHMARK returns are net of withholding taxes if this information is available.

  

**4.C.27** If the GIPS COMPOSITE REPORT conforms with laws and/or regulations that conflict with the REQUIREMENTS of the GIPS standards, the FIRM MUST disclose this fact and disclose the manner in which the laws and/or regulations conflict with the GIPS standards.

**4.C.28** If CARVE-OUTS with allocated cash are included in the COMPOSITE, the FIRM MUST:

a. Indicate CARVE-OUT in the COMPOSITE name.

b. Disclose that the COMPOSITE includes CARVE-OUTS with allocated cash.

c. Disclose the policy used to allocate cash to CARVE-OUTS.

d. Disclose that the GIPS COMPOSITE REPORT for the COMPOSITE of standalone PORTFOLIOS is available upon request, if the COMPOSITE of standalone PORTFOLIOS exists.

**4.C.29** The FIRM MUST disclose the use of a SUB-ADVISOR and the periods a SUB-ADVISOR was used.[35]

**4.C.30** The FIRM MUST disclose if the COMPOSITE'S valuation hierarchy materially differs from the RECOMMENDED valuation hierarchy. (See provision 2.B.6 for the RECOMMENDED valuation hierarchy.)[36]

**4.C.31** If the FIRM determines no appropriate BENCHMARK for the COMPOSITE exists, the FIRM MUST disclose why no BENCHMARK is presented.

**4.C.32** If the FIRM changes the BENCHMARK, the FIRM MUST disclose:

a. For a prospective BENCHMARK change, the date and description of the change. Changes MUST be disclosed for as long as returns for the prior BENCHMARK are included in the GIPS COMPOSITE REPORT.

b. For a retroactive BENCHMARK change, the date and description of the change. Changes MUST be disclosed for a minimum of one year and for as long as they are relevant to interpreting the track record.

**4.C.33** If a custom BENCHMARK or combination of multiple BENCHMARKS is used, the FIRM MUST:

a. Disclose the BENCHMARK components, weights, and rebalancing process, if applicable.

b. Disclose the calculation methodology.

c. Clearly label the BENCHMARK to indicate that it is a custom BENCHMARK.

**4.C.34** If a PORTFOLIO-WEIGHTED CUSTOM BENCHMARK is used, the FIRM MUST disclose:

a. That the BENCHMARK is rebalanced using the weighted average returns of the BENCHMARKS of all of the PORTFOLIOS included in the COMPOSITE.

b. The frequency of the rebalancing.

---

[35] REQUIRED for periods beginning on or after 1 January 2006.

[36] REQUIRED for periods beginning on or after 1 January 2011.

c. The components that constitute the PORTFOLIO-WEIGHTED CUSTOM BENCHMARK, including the weights that each component represents, as of the most recent annual period end.

d. That the components that constitute the PORTFOLIO-WEIGHTED CUSTOM BENCHMARK, including the weights that each component represents, are available for prior periods upon request.

**4.C.35** If the FIRM has adopted a SIGNIFICANT CASH FLOW policy for the COMPOSITE, the FIRM MUST disclose how the FIRM defines a SIGNIFICANT CASH FLOW for the COMPOSITE and for which periods.

**4.C.36** For COMPOSITES with at least three annual periods of performance, the FIRM MUST disclose if the three-year annualized EX POST STANDARD DEVIATION of the COMPOSITE and/or BENCHMARK is not presented because 36 monthly returns are not available.

**4.C.37** The FIRM MUST disclose if performance from a past firm or affiliation is presented, and for which periods.

**4.C.38** The FIRM MUST disclose any change to the GIPS COMPOSITE REPORT resulting from the correction of a MATERIAL ERROR. Following the correction of the GIPS COMPOSITE REPORT, this disclosure MUST be included for a minimum of one year and for as long as it is relevant to interpreting the track record. This disclosure is not REQUIRED to be included in a GIPS COMPOSITE REPORT that is provided to a PROSPECTIVE CLIENT or PROSPECTIVE INVESTOR that did not receive the GIPS COMPOSITE REPORT containing the MATERIAL ERROR.

**4.C.39** If the FIRM chooses to not present the number of PORTFOLIOS in the COMPOSITE because there are five or fewer PORTFOLIOS in the COMPOSITE, the FIRM MUST disclose that the COMPOSITE contains five or fewer PORTFOLIOS or use similar language.

**4.C.40** If the FIRM chooses to not present the INTERNAL DISPERSION of individual PORTFOLIO returns because there are five or fewer PORTFOLIOS in the COMPOSITE for the full year, the FIRM MUST disclose that the INTERNAL DISPERSION measure is not applicable or use similar language.

**4.C.41** The FIRM MUST disclose if preliminary, estimated values are used to determine FAIR VALUE.

**4.C.42** If the FIRM changes the type of return(s) presented for the COMPOSITE (e.g., changes from MONEY-WEIGHTED RETURNS to TIME-WEIGHTED RETURNS), the FIRM MUST disclose the change and the date of the change. This disclosure MUST be included for a minimum of one year and for as long as it is relevant to interpreting the track record.

**4.C.43** If the FIRM presents ADDITIONAL RISK MEASURES, the FIRM MUST:

a. Describe any ADDITIONAL RISK MEASURE.

b. Disclose the name of the risk-free rate if a risk-free rate is used in the calculation of the ADDITIONAL RISK MEASURE.

  

4.C.44 The FIRM MUST disclose if GROSS-OF-FEES or NET-OF-FEES returns are used to calculate presented risk measures.

4.C.45 For OVERLAY STRATEGY COMPOSITES, the FIRM MUST disclose:

a. The methodology used to calculate COMPOSITE OVERLAY EXPOSURE.

b. If collateral and collateral income are reflected in the COMPOSITE returns.

4.C.46 For REAL ESTATE investments that are not in a REAL ESTATE OPEN-END FUND, the FIRM MUST disclose that:[37]

a. EXTERNAL VALUATIONS are obtained, and the frequency with which they are obtained, or

b. The FIRM relies on valuations from financial statement audits.

4.C.47 For WRAP FEE COMPOSITES, when the FIRM presents PURE GROSS-OF-FEES returns, the FIRM MUST disclose that PURE GROSS-OF-FEES returns do not reflect the deduction of TRANSACTION COSTS.

4.C.48 When the GIPS COMPOSITE REPORT includes THEORETICAL PERFORMANCE as SUPPLEMENTAL INFORMATION, the FIRM MUST:

a. Disclose that the results are theoretical, are not based on the performance of actual assets, and if the THEORETICAL PERFORMANCE was derived from the retroactive or prospective application of a model.

b. Disclose a basic description of the methodology and assumptions used to calculate the THEORETICAL PERFORMANCE sufficient for the PROSPECTIVE CLIENT or PROSPECTIVE INVESTOR to interpret the THEORETICAL PERFORMANCE, including if it is based on model performance, backtested performance, or hypothetical performance.

c. Disclose whether the THEORETICAL PERFORMANCE reflects the deduction of actual or estimated INVESTMENT MANAGEMENT FEES, TRANSACTION COSTS, or other fees and charges that an actual client PORTFOLIO would have paid or will pay.

d. Clearly label the THEORETICAL PERFORMANCE as SUPPLEMENTAL INFORMATION.

## 4.D. Disclosure—Recommendations

4.D.1 The FIRM SHOULD disclose material changes to valuation policies and/or methodologies.

4.D.2 The FIRM SHOULD disclose material changes to calculation policies and/or methodologies.

4.D.3 The FIRM SHOULD disclose material differences between the BENCHMARK and the COMPOSITE's investment mandate, objective, or strategy.

4.D.4 The FIRM SHOULD disclose the key assumptions used to value investments.

[37] REQUIRED for periods ending on or after 31 December 2020.

  

**4.D.5** If a parent company contains multiple firms, each FIRM within the parent company SHOULD disclose a list of the other firms contained within the parent company.

**4.D.6** If the COMPOSITE contains PORTFOLIOS with BUNDLED FEES, the FIRM SHOULD disclose the types of fees included in the BUNDLED FEE.

**4.D.7** If the FIRM adheres to any industry valuation guidelines in addition to the GIPS valuation REQUIREMENTS, the FIRM SHOULD disclose which guidelines have been applied.

**4.D.8** When using BENCHMARKS that have limitations, such as peer group BENCHMARKS, the FIRM SHOULD disclose these limitations.

**4.D.9** The FIRM SHOULD disclose how research costs are reflected in returns.

  

# 5. COMPOSITE MONEY-WEIGHTED RETURN REPORT

**The following provisions apply to COMPOSITES that include MONEY-WEIGHTED RETURNS in a GIPS COMPOSITE REPORT when the FIRM meets the REQUIREMENTS specified in provision 1.A.35 and chooses to present MONEY-WEIGHTED RETURNS.**

## 5.A. Presentation and Reporting—Requirements

5.A.1 The FIRM MUST present in each GIPS COMPOSITE REPORT:

a. The annualized COMPOSITE SINCE-INCEPTION MONEY-WEIGHTED RETURN through the most recent annual period end.

b. When the COMPOSITE has a track record that is less than a full year, the non-annualized COMPOSITE SINCE-INCEPTION MONEY-WEIGHTED RETURN through the initial annual period end.

c. When the COMPOSITE terminates, the annualized COMPOSITE SINCE-INCEPTION MONEY-WEIGHTED RETURN through the COMPOSITE TERMINATION DATE.

d. The SINCE-INCEPTION MONEY-WEIGHTED RETURN for the BENCHMARK for the same periods as presented for the COMPOSITE, unless the FIRM determines there is no appropriate BENCHMARK.

e. The number of PORTFOLIOS in the COMPOSITE as of the most recent annual period end. If the COMPOSITE contains five or fewer PORTFOLIOS at period end, the number of PORTFOLIOS is not REQUIRED.

f. COMPOSITE assets as of the most recent annual period end.

g. TOTAL FIRM ASSETS as of the most recent annual period end.[38]

5.A.2 If a SUBSCRIPTION LINE OF CREDIT is used, the FIRM MUST present the COMPOSITE SINCE-INCEPTION MONEY-WEIGHTED RETURN both with and without the SUBSCRIPTION LINE OF CREDIT through the most recent annual period end. The FIRM is not REQUIRED to present returns without the SUBSCRIPTION LINE OF CREDIT when the SUBSCRIPTION LINE OF CREDIT has all of the following characteristics:[39]

a. The principal was repaid within 120 days using COMMITTED CAPITAL drawn down through a capital call.

b. No principal was used to fund DISTRIBUTIONS.

---

[38] REQUIRED for periods ending on or after 31 December 2020. For periods ending prior to 31 December 2020, FIRMS may present either TOTAL FIRM ASSETS or COMPOSITE assets as a percentage of TOTAL FIRM ASSETS.

[39] REQUIRED for periods ending on or after 31 December 2020.

**5.A.3** The FIRM MUST present the percentage of the total FAIR VALUE of COMPOSITE assets that were valued using subjective, unobservable inputs (as described in provision 2.B.6.e) as of the most recent annual period end, if such investments represent a material amount of COMPOSITE assets.

**5.A.4** If PORTFOLIOS in the COMPOSITE have COMMITTED CAPITAL, the FIRM MUST present the following items as of the most recent annual period end:

a. COMPOSITE SINCE-INCEPTION PAID-IN CAPITAL.

b. COMPOSITE SINCE-INCEPTION DISTRIBUTIONS.

c. COMPOSITE cumulative COMMITTED CAPITAL.

d. TOTAL VALUE to SINCE-INCEPTION PAID-IN CAPITAL (INVESTMENT MULTIPLE or TVPI).

e. SINCE-INCEPTION DISTRIBUTIONS to SINCE-INCEPTION PAID-IN CAPITAL (REALIZATION MULTIPLE or DPI).

f. SINCE-INCEPTION PAID-IN CAPITAL to cumulative COMMITTED CAPITAL (PIC MULTIPLE).

g. RESIDUAL VALUE to SINCE-INCEPTION PAID-IN CAPITAL (UNREALIZED MULTIPLE or RVPI).

**5.A.5** The FIRM MUST clearly label or identify:

a. The periods that are presented.

b. If COMPOSITE returns are GROSS-OF-FEES or NET-OF-FEES.

c. If COMPOSITE returns do or do not reflect the SUBSCRIPTION LINE OF CREDIT. This information is REQUIRED only if the FIRM presents returns both with and without the SUBSCRIPTION LINE OF CREDIT.

**5.A.6** If the FIRM includes more than one BENCHMARK in the GIPS COMPOSITE REPORT, the FIRM MUST present and disclose all REQUIRED information for all BENCHMARKS presented.

**5.A.7** If the COMPOSITE includes CARVE-OUTS with allocated cash, the FIRM MUST present the percentage of COMPOSITE assets represented by CARVE-OUTS with allocated cash as of the most recent annual period end.

**5.A.8** If the COMPOSITE includes non-fee-paying PORTFOLIOS, the FIRM MUST present the percentage of COMPOSITE assets represented by non-fee-paying PORTFOLIOS as of the most recent annual period end when NET-OF-FEES returns are presented and are calculated using actual INVESTMENT MANAGEMENT FEES.

**5.A.9** If the FIRM chooses to present COMPOSITE uncalled COMMITTED CAPITAL or a combination of COMPOSITE assets and COMPOSITE uncalled COMMITTED CAPITAL, the FIRM MUST:

a. Present COMPOSITE uncalled COMMITTED CAPITAL for the same periods for which the combination of COMPOSITE assets and COMPOSITE uncalled COMMITTED CAPITAL is presented.

  

b. Clearly label COMPOSITE uncalled COMMITTED CAPITAL as such.

c. Clearly label the combination of COMPOSITE assets and COMPOSITE uncalled COMMITTED CAPITAL as such.

5.A.10 If the FIRM chooses to present FIRM-wide uncalled COMMITTED CAPITAL or a combination of TOTAL FIRM ASSETS and FIRM-wide uncalled COMMITTED CAPITAL, the FIRM MUST:

a. Present FIRM-wide uncalled COMMITTED CAPITAL for the same periods for which the combination of TOTAL FIRM ASSETS and FIRM-wide uncalled COMMITTED CAPITAL is presented.

b. Clearly label FIRM-wide uncalled COMMITTED CAPITAL as such.

c. Clearly label the combination of TOTAL FIRM ASSETS and FIRM-wide uncalled COMMITTED CAPITAL as such.

5.A.11 If the FIRM chooses to present ADVISORY-ONLY ASSETS that reflect the COMPOSITE'S investment mandate, objective, or strategy or a combination of COMPOSITE assets and ADVISORY-ONLY ASSETS that reflect the COMPOSITE'S investment mandate, objective, or strategy, the FIRM MUST:

a. Present ADVISORY-ONLY ASSETS that reflect the COMPOSITE'S investment mandate, objective, or strategy for the same periods for which the combination of COMPOSITE assets and ADVISORY-ONLY ASSETS that reflect the COMPOSITE'S investment mandate, objective, or strategy is presented.

b. Clearly label ADVISORY-ONLY ASSETS that reflect the COMPOSITE'S investment mandate, objective, or strategy as such.

c. Clearly label the combination of COMPOSITE assets and ADVISORY-ONLY ASSETS that reflect the COMPOSITE'S investment mandate, objective, or strategy as such.

5.A.12 If the FIRM chooses to present FIRM-wide ADVISORY-ONLY ASSETS or a combination of TOTAL FIRM ASSETS and FIRM-wide ADVISORY-ONLY ASSETS, the FIRM MUST:

a. Present FIRM-wide ADVISORY-ONLY ASSETS for the same periods for which the combination of TOTAL FIRM ASSETS and FIRM-wide ADVISORY-ONLY ASSETS is presented.

b. Clearly label FIRM-wide ADVISORY-ONLY ASSETS as such.

c. Clearly label the combination of TOTAL FIRM ASSETS and FIRM-wide ADVISORY-ONLY ASSETS as such.

5.A.13 All REQUIRED and RECOMMENDED information in the GIPS COMPOSITE REPORT MUST be presented in the same currency.

5.A.14 When the FIRM presents the performance of a COMPOSITE that includes CARVE-OUTS with allocated cash and also has a COMPOSITE of standalone PORTFOLIOS managed according to the same strategy, the FIRM MUST present the COMPOSITE SINCE-INCEPTION MONEY-WEIGHTED RETURN through the most recent annual period end and the COMPOSITE assets of the COMPOSITE of standalone PORTFOLIOS as of the most recent annual period end in the GIPS COMPOSITE REPORT of the COMPOSITE that includes CARVE-OUTS with allocated cash.

5.A.15 Any SUPPLEMENTAL INFORMATION included in the GIPS COMPOSITE REPORT:

a. MUST relate directly to the COMPOSITE.

b. MUST NOT contradict or conflict with the REQUIRED or RECOMMENDED information in the GIPS COMPOSITE REPORT.

c. MUST be clearly labeled as SUPPLEMENTAL INFORMATION.

## 5.B. Presentation and Reporting—Recommendations

5.B.1 The FIRM SHOULD present annualized SINCE-INCEPTION MONEY-WEIGHTED RETURNS as of each annual period end.

5.B.2 If PORTFOLIOS in the COMPOSITE have COMMITTED CAPITAL, the FIRM SHOULD present the following items as of each annual period end:

a. COMPOSITE SINCE-INCEPTION PAID-IN CAPITAL.

b. COMPOSITE SINCE-INCEPTION DISTRIBUTIONS.

c. COMPOSITE cumulative COMMITTED CAPITAL.

d. TOTAL VALUE to SINCE-INCEPTION PAID-IN CAPITAL (INVESTMENT MULTIPLE or TVPI).

e. SINCE-INCEPTION DISTRIBUTIONS to SINCE-INCEPTION PAID-IN CAPITAL (REALIZATION MULTIPLE or DPI).

f. SINCE-INCEPTION PAID-IN CAPITAL to cumulative COMMITTED CAPITAL (PIC MULTIPLE).

g. RESIDUAL VALUE to SINCE-INCEPTION PAID-IN CAPITAL (UNREALIZED MULTIPLE or RVPI).

5.B.3 The FIRM SHOULD present both annualized GROSS-OF-FEES and NET-OF-FEES COMPOSITE SINCE-INCEPTION MONEY-WEIGHTED RETURNS.

5.B.4 The FIRM SHOULD present PROPRIETARY ASSETS as a percentage of COMPOSITE assets as of the most recent annual period end.

5.B.5 The FIRM SHOULD present an appropriate EX POST risk measure for the COMPOSITE and the BENCHMARK. The same EX POST risk measure SHOULD be presented for the COMPOSITE and the BENCHMARK.

5.B.6 If the FIRM uses preliminary, estimated values as FAIR VALUE, the FIRM SHOULD present the percentage of assets in the COMPOSITE that were valued using preliminary, estimated values as of the most recent annual period end.

  

5.B.7 If the FIRM has COMMITTED CAPITAL, the FIRM SHOULD present FIRM-wide uncalled COMMITTED CAPITAL as of the most recent annual period end.

## 5.C. Disclosure—Requirements

5.C.1 Once the FIRM has met all the applicable REQUIREMENTS of the GIPS standards, the FIRM MUST disclose its compliance with the GIPS standards using one of the following compliance statements. The compliance statement for a COMPOSITE MUST only be used in a GIPS COMPOSITE REPORT.

a. For a FIRM that is verified:

> "[Insert name of FIRM] claims compliance with the Global Investment Performance Standards (GIPS®) and has prepared and presented this report in compliance with the GIPS standards. [Insert name of FIRM] has been independently verified for the periods [insert dates]. The verification report(s) is/are available upon request.
>
> "A firm that claims compliance with the GIPS standards must establish policies and procedures for complying with all the applicable requirements of the GIPS standards. Verification provides assurance on whether the firm's policies and procedures related to composite and pooled fund maintenance, as well as the calculation, presentation, and distribution of performance, have been designed in compliance with the GIPS standards and have been implemented on a firm-wide basis. Verification does not provide assurance on the accuracy of any specific performance report."

b. For COMPOSITES of a verified FIRM that have also had a PERFORMANCE EXAMINATION:

> "[Insert name of FIRM] claims compliance with the Global Investment Performance Standards (GIPS®) and has prepared and presented this report in compliance with the GIPS standards. [Insert name of FIRM] has been independently verified for the periods [insert dates].
>
> "A firm that claims compliance with the GIPS standards must establish policies and procedures for complying with all the applicable requirements of the GIPS standards. Verification provides assurance on whether the firm's policies and procedures related to composite and pooled fund maintenance, as well as the calculation, presentation, and distribution of performance, have been designed in compliance with the GIPS standards and have been implemented on a firm-wide basis. The [insert name of COMPOSITE] has had a performance examination for the periods [insert dates]. The verification and performance examination reports are available upon request."

The compliance statement for a FIRM that is verified or for COMPOSITES of a verified FIRM that have also had a PERFORMANCE EXAMINATION is complete only when both paragraphs are shown together, one after the other.

c. For a FIRM that has not been verified:

> "[Insert name of FIRM] claims compliance with the Global Investment Performance Standards (GIPS®) and has prepared and presented this report in compliance with the GIPS standards. [Insert name of FIRM] has not been independently verified."

The FIRM MUST NOT exclude any portion of the respective compliance statement. Any modifications to the compliance statement MUST be additive.

**5.C.2** The FIRM MUST disclose the following: "GIPS® is a registered trademark of CFA Institute. CFA Institute does not endorse or promote this organization, nor does it warrant the accuracy or quality of the content contained herein."

**5.C.3** The FIRM MUST disclose the definition of the FIRM used to determine TOTAL FIRM ASSETS and FIRM-wide compliance.

**5.C.4** The FIRM MUST disclose the COMPOSITE DESCRIPTION.

**5.C.5** The FIRM MUST disclose the BENCHMARK DESCRIPTION, which MUST include the key features of the BENCHMARK or the name of the BENCHMARK for a readily recognized index or other point of reference.

**5.C.6** When presenting GROSS-OF-FEES returns, the FIRM MUST disclose if any other fees are deducted in addition to TRANSACTION COSTS.

**5.C.7** When presenting NET-OF-FEES returns, the FIRM MUST disclose:

a. If any other fees are deducted in addition to INVESTMENT MANAGEMENT FEES and TRANSACTION COSTS.

b. If NET-OF-FEES returns are net of any PERFORMANCE-BASED FEES or CARRIED INTEREST.

c. If model or actual INVESTMENT MANAGEMENT FEES are used.

d. If model INVESTMENT MANAGEMENT FEES are used and COMPOSITE GROSS-OF-FEES returns are not presented, the model INVESTMENT MANAGEMENT FEE used to calculate NET-OF-FEES returns.[40]

e. If model INVESTMENT MANAGEMENT FEES are used, the methodology used to calculate NET-OF-FEES returns.

**5.C.8** The FIRM MUST disclose which fees and expenses other than INVESTMENT MANAGEMENT FEES (e.g., research costs) are separately charged by the FIRM to clients, if material.

**5.C.9** The FIRM MUST disclose or otherwise indicate the reporting currency.

[40] REQUIRED for periods ending on or after 31 December 2020.

  

**5.C.10** The FIRM MUST disclose the current FEE SCHEDULE appropriate to PROSPECTIVE CLIENTS or PROSPECTIVE INVESTORS.

a. When presenting performance to a PROSPECTIVE CLIENT for a standalone PORTFOLIO, the FEE SCHEDULE MUST reflect the FEE SCHEDULE for a standalone PORTFOLIO managed according to that strategy.

b. When presenting performance of a COMPOSITE that includes CARVE-OUTS to a PROSPECTIVE CLIENT for a multi-asset strategy PORTFOLIO, the FEE SCHEDULE MUST reflect the FEE SCHEDULE for a multi-asset strategy PORTFOLIO managed according to that strategy.

c. When presenting a GIPS COMPOSITE REPORT to a PROSPECTIVE INVESTOR for a POOLED FUND included in the COMPOSITE, the FIRM MUST disclose the POOLED FUND'S current FEE SCHEDULE and EXPENSE RATIO.

**5.C.11** If the FEE SCHEDULE includes PERFORMANCE-BASED FEES or CARRIED INTEREST, the FIRM MUST disclose the PERFORMANCE-BASED FEE DESCRIPTION or CARRIED INTEREST DESCRIPTION.

**5.C.12** The FIRM MUST disclose the COMPOSITE INCEPTION DATE.

**5.C.13** The FIRM MUST disclose the COMPOSITE CREATION DATE.

**5.C.14** The FIRM MUST disclose that the following lists are available upon request, if applicable:

a. List of COMPOSITE DESCRIPTIONS.

b. List of POOLED FUND DESCRIPTIONS for LIMITED DISTRIBUTION POOLED FUNDS.

c. List of BROAD DISTRIBUTION POOLED FUNDS.

**5.C.15** The FIRM MUST disclose that policies for valuing investments, calculating performance, and preparing GIPS REPORTS are available upon request.

**5.C.16** The FIRM MUST disclose how leverage, derivatives, and short positions have been used historically, if material.

**5.C.17** If estimated TRANSACTION COSTS are used, the FIRM MUST disclose:

a. That estimated TRANSACTION COSTS were used.

b. The estimated TRANSACTION COSTS used and how they were determined.

**5.C.18** The FIRM MUST disclose all significant events that would help a PROSPECTIVE CLIENT interpret the GIPS COMPOSITE REPORT. This disclosure MUST be included for a minimum of one year and for as long as it is relevant to interpreting the track record.

**5.C.19** For any performance presented for periods prior to the MINIMUM EFFECTIVE COMPLIANCE DATE that does not comply with the GIPS standards, the FIRM MUST disclose the periods of non-compliance.

**5.C.20** If the FIRM is redefined, the FIRM MUST disclose the date and description of the redefinition.

  

**5.C.21** If the COMPOSITE is redefined, the FIRM MUST disclose the date and description of the redefinition.

**5.C.22** The FIRM MUST disclose changes to the name of the COMPOSITE. This disclosure MUST be included for a minimum of one year and for as long as it is relevant to interpreting the track record.

**5.C.23** The FIRM MUST disclose:

a. The minimum asset level, if any, below which PORTFOLIOS are not included in the COMPOSITE.

b. Any changes to the minimum asset level.

**5.C.24** The FIRM MUST disclose if COMPOSITE returns are gross or net of withholding taxes, if material.

**5.C.25** The FIRM MUST disclose if BENCHMARK returns are net of withholding taxes if this information is available.

**5.C.26** If the GIPS COMPOSITE REPORT conforms with laws and/or regulations that conflict with the REQUIREMENTS of the GIPS standards, the FIRM MUST disclose this fact and disclose the manner in which the laws and/or regulations conflict with the GIPS standards.

**5.C.27** If CARVE-OUTS with allocated cash are included in the COMPOSITE, the FIRM MUST:

a. Indicate CARVE-OUT in the COMPOSITE name.

b. Disclose that the COMPOSITE includes CARVE-OUTS with allocated cash.

c. Disclose the policy used to allocate cash to CARVE-OUTS.

d. Disclose that the GIPS COMPOSITE REPORT for the COMPOSITE of standalone PORTFOLIOS is available upon request, if the COMPOSITE of standalone PORTFOLIOS exists.

**5.C.28** The FIRM MUST disclose the use of a SUB-ADVISOR and the periods a SUB-ADVISOR was used.[41]

**5.C.29** The FIRM MUST disclose if the COMPOSITE'S valuation hierarchy materially differs from the RECOMMENDED valuation hierarchy. (See provision 2.B.6 for the RECOMMENDED valuation hierarchy.)[42]

**5.C.30** If the FIRM determines no appropriate BENCHMARK for the COMPOSITE exists, the FIRM MUST disclose why no BENCHMARK is presented.

**5.C.31** If the FIRM changes the BENCHMARK, the FIRM MUST disclose:

a. For a prospective BENCHMARK change, the date and description of the change. Changes MUST be disclosed for as long as returns for the prior BENCHMARK are included in the GIPS COMPOSITE REPORT.

---

[41] REQUIRED for periods beginning on or after 1 January 2006.

[42] REQUIRED for periods beginning on or after 1 January 2011.

  

b. For a retroactive BENCHMARK change, the date and description of the change. Changes MUST be disclosed for a minimum of one year and for as long as they are relevant to interpreting the track record.

5.C.32 If a custom BENCHMARK or combination of multiple BENCHMARKS is used, the FIRM MUST:

a. Disclose the BENCHMARK components, weights, and rebalancing process, if applicable.

b. Disclose the calculation methodology.

c. Clearly label the BENCHMARK to indicate that it is a custom BENCHMARK.

5.C.33 The FIRM MUST disclose the calculation methodology used for the BENCHMARK. If the FIRM presents the PUBLIC MARKET EQUIVALENT of the COMPOSITE as a BENCHMARK, the FIRM MUST also disclose the index used to calculate the PUBLIC MARKET EQUIVALENT.

5.C.34 The FIRM MUST disclose if performance from a past firm or affiliation is presented, and for which periods.

5.C.35 The FIRM MUST disclose the frequency of EXTERNAL CASH FLOWS used in the MONEY-WEIGHTED RETURN calculation if daily frequency was not used.

5.C.36 If a SUBSCRIPTION LINE OF CREDIT is used, and the FIRM is REQUIRED to present returns both with and without the SUBSCRIPTION LINE OF CREDIT, the FIRM MUST disclose:

a. The purpose for using the SUBSCRIPTION LINE OF CREDIT.

b. The size of the SUBSCRIPTION LINE OF CREDIT as of the most recent annual period end.

c. The SUBSCRIPTION LINE OF CREDIT amount outstanding as of the most recent annual period end.

5.C.37 The FIRM MUST disclose any change to the GIPS COMPOSITE REPORT resulting from the correction of a MATERIAL ERROR. Following the correction of the GIPS COMPOSITE REPORT, this disclosure MUST be included for a minimum of one year and for as long as it is relevant to interpreting the track record. This disclosure is not REQUIRED to be included in a GIPS COMPOSITE REPORT that is provided to a PROSPECTIVE CLIENT or PROSPECTIVE INVESTOR that did not receive the GIPS COMPOSITE REPORT containing the MATERIAL ERROR.

5.C.38 If the FIRM chooses to not present the number of PORTFOLIOS in the COMPOSITE because there are five or fewer PORTFOLIOS in the COMPOSITE, the FIRM MUST disclose that the COMPOSITE contains five or fewer PORTFOLIOS or use similar language.

5.C.39 The FIRM MUST disclose if preliminary, estimated values are used to determine FAIR VALUE.

5.C.40 If the FIRM changes the type of return(s) presented for the COMPOSITE (e.g., changes from TIME-WEIGHTED RETURNS to MONEY-WEIGHTED RETURNS), the FIRM MUST disclose the change and the date of the change. This disclosure MUST be included for a minimum of one year and for as long as it is relevant to interpreting the track record.

**5.C.41** If the FIRM presents ADDITIONAL RISK MEASURES, the FIRM MUST:

a. Describe any ADDITIONAL RISK MEASURE.

b. Disclose the name of the risk-free rate if a risk-free rate is used in the calculation of the ADDITIONAL RISK MEASURE.

**5.C.42** The FIRM MUST disclose if GROSS-OF-FEES or NET-OF-FEES returns are used to calculate presented risk measures.

**5.C.43** For REAL ESTATE investments that are not in a REAL ESTATE OPEN-END FUND, the FIRM MUST disclose that:[43]

a. EXTERNAL VALUATIONS are obtained, and the frequency with which they are obtained, or

b. The FIRM relies on valuations from financial statement audits.

**5.C.44** When the GIPS COMPOSITE REPORT includes THEORETICAL PERFORMANCE as SUPPLEMENTAL INFORMATION, the FIRM MUST:

a. Disclose that the results are theoretical, are not based on the performance of actual assets, and if the THEORETICAL PERFORMANCE was derived from the retroactive or prospective application of a model.

b. Disclose a basic description of the methodology and assumptions used to calculate the THEORETICAL PERFORMANCE sufficient for the PROSPECTIVE CLIENT or PROSPECTIVE INVESTOR to interpret the THEORETICAL PERFORMANCE, including if it is based on model performance, backtested performance, or hypothetical performance.

c. Disclose whether the THEORETICAL PERFORMANCE reflects the deduction of actual or estimated INVESTMENT MANAGEMENT FEES, TRANSACTION COSTS, or other fees and charges that an actual client PORTFOLIO would have paid or will pay.

d. Clearly label the THEORETICAL PERFORMANCE as SUPPLEMENTAL INFORMATION.

## 5.D. Disclosure—Recommendations

**5.D.1** The FIRM SHOULD disclose material changes to valuation policies and/or methodologies.

**5.D.2** The FIRM SHOULD disclose material changes to calculation policies and/or methodologies.

**5.D.3** The FIRM SHOULD disclose material differences between the BENCHMARK and the COMPOSITE'S investment mandate, objective, or strategy.

**5.D.4** The FIRM SHOULD disclose the key assumptions used to value investments.

**5.D.5** If a parent company contains multiple firms, each FIRM within the parent company SHOULD disclose a list of the other firms contained within the parent company.

---

[43] REQUIRED for periods ending on or after 31 December 2020.

  

5.D.6 If the COMPOSITE contains PORTFOLIOS with BUNDLED FEES, the FIRM SHOULD disclose the types of fees included in the BUNDLED FEE.

5.D.7 If the FIRM adheres to any industry valuation guidelines in addition to the GIPS valuation REQUIREMENTS, the FIRM SHOULD disclose which guidelines have been applied.

5.D.8 When using BENCHMARKS that have limitations, such as peer group BENCHMARKS, the FIRM SHOULD disclose these limitations.

5.D.9 The FIRM SHOULD disclose how research costs are reflected in returns.

# 6. POOLED FUND TIME-WEIGHTED RETURN REPORT

**The following provisions apply to POOLED FUNDS that include TIME-WEIGHTED RETURNS in a GIPS POOLED FUND REPORT.**

## 6.A. Presentation and Reporting—Requirements

6.A.1 The FIRM MUST present in each GIPS POOLED FUND REPORT:

a. At least five years of performance (or for the period since the POOLED FUND INCEPTION DATE if the POOLED FUND has been in existence less than five years) that meets the REQUIREMENTS of the GIPS standards. After the FIRM presents a minimum of five years of GIPS-compliant performance (or for the period since the POOLED FUND INCEPTION DATE if the POOLED FUND has been in existence less than five years), the FIRM MUST present an additional year of performance each year, building up to a minimum of 10 years of GIPS-compliant performance.

b. POOLED FUND returns for each annual period.

c. When the initial period is less than a full year, the return from the POOLED FUND INCEPTION DATE through the initial annual period end.[44]

d. When the POOLED FUND terminates, the return from the last annual period end through the POOLED FUND TERMINATION DATE.[45]

e. The TOTAL RETURN for the BENCHMARK for each annual period and for all other periods for which POOLED FUND returns are presented, unless the FIRM determines there is no appropriate BENCHMARK.

f. POOLED FUND assets as of each annual period end.

g. TOTAL FIRM ASSETS as of each annual period end.[46]

h. For POOLED FUNDS for which monthly POOLED FUND returns are available, the three-year annualized EX POST STANDARD DEVIATION (using monthly returns) of the POOLED FUND and the BENCHMARK as of each annual period end.[47]

[44] REQUIRED for POOLED FUNDS with a POOLED FUND INCEPTION DATE of 1 January 2011 or later.

[45] REQUIRED for POOLED FUNDS with a POOLED FUND TERMINATION DATE of 1 January 2011 or later.

[46] REQUIRED for periods ending on or after 31 December 2020. For periods ending prior to 31 December 2020, FIRMS may present either TOTAL FIRM ASSETS or POOLED FUND assets as a percentage of TOTAL FIRM ASSETS.

[47] REQUIRED for periods ending on or after 1 January 2011.

 

6.A.2 The FIRM MUST present the percentage of the total FAIR VALUE of POOLED FUND assets that were valued using subjective unobservable inputs (as described in provision 2.B.6.e) as of the most recent annual period end, if such investments represent a material amount of POOLED FUND assets.

6.A.3 The FIRM MUST clearly label or identify:

a. The periods that are presented.

b. If POOLED FUND returns are POOLED FUND GROSS RETURNS or POOLED FUND NET RETURNS.

6.A.4 If the FIRM includes more than one BENCHMARK in the GIPS POOLED FUND REPORT, the FIRM MUST present and disclose all REQUIRED information for all BENCHMARKS presented.

6.A.5 The FIRM MUST present the POOLED FUND EXPENSE RATIO appropriate to PROSPECTIVE INVESTORS.

6.A.6 If the FIRM chooses to present POOLED FUND uncalled COMMITTED CAPITAL or a combination of POOLED FUND assets and POOLED FUND uncalled COMMITTED CAPITAL, the FIRM MUST:

a. Present POOLED FUND uncalled COMMITTED CAPITAL for the same periods for which the combination of POOLED FUND assets and POOLED FUND uncalled COMMITTED CAPITAL is presented.

b. Clearly label POOLED FUND uncalled COMMITTED CAPITAL as such.

c. Clearly label the combination of POOLED FUND assets and POOLED FUND uncalled COMMITTED CAPITAL as such.

6.A.7 If the FIRM chooses to present FIRM-wide uncalled COMMITTED CAPITAL or a combination of TOTAL FIRM ASSETS and FIRM-wide uncalled COMMITTED CAPITAL, the FIRM MUST:

a. Present FIRM-wide uncalled COMMITTED CAPITAL for the same periods for which the combination of TOTAL FIRM ASSETS and FIRM-wide uncalled COMMITTED CAPITAL is presented.

b. Clearly label FIRM-wide uncalled COMMITTED CAPITAL as such.

c. Clearly label the combination of TOTAL FIRM ASSETS and FIRM-wide uncalled COMMITTED CAPITAL as such.

6.A.8 If the FIRM chooses to present ADVISORY-ONLY ASSETS that reflect the POOLED FUND'S investment mandate, objective, or strategy or a combination of POOLED FUND assets and ADVISORY-ONLY ASSETS that reflect the POOLED FUND'S investment mandate, objective, or strategy, the FIRM MUST:

a. Present ADVISORY-ONLY ASSETS that reflect the POOLED FUND'S investment mandate, objective, or strategy for the same periods for which the combination of POOLED FUND assets and ADVISORY-ONLY ASSETS that reflect the POOLED FUND'S investment mandate, objective, or strategy is presented.

b. Clearly label ADVISORY-ONLY ASSETS that reflect the POOLED FUND'S investment mandate, objective, or strategy as such.

c. Clearly label the combination of POOLED FUND assets and ADVISORY-ONLY ASSETS that reflect the POOLED FUND'S investment mandate, objective, or strategy as such.

6.A.9 If the FIRM chooses to present FIRM-wide ADVISORY-ONLY ASSETS or a combination of TOTAL FIRM ASSETS and FIRM-wide ADVISORY-ONLY ASSETS, the FIRM MUST:

a. Present FIRM-wide ADVISORY-ONLY ASSETS for the same periods for which the combination of TOTAL FIRM ASSETS and FIRM-wide ADVISORY-ONLY ASSETS is presented.

b. Clearly label FIRM-wide ADVISORY-ONLY ASSETS as such.

c. Clearly label the combination of TOTAL FIRM ASSETS and FIRM-wide ADVISORY-ONLY ASSETS as such.

6.A.10 All REQUIRED and RECOMMENDED information in the GIPS POOLED FUND REPORT MUST be presented in the same currency.

6.A.11 Any SUPPLEMENTAL INFORMATION included in the GIPS POOLED FUND REPORT:

a. MUST relate directly to the POOLED FUND.

b. MUST NOT contradict or conflict with the REQUIRED or RECOMMENDED information in the GIPS POOLED FUND REPORT.

c. MUST be clearly labeled as SUPPLEMENTAL INFORMATION.

## 6.B. Presentation and Reporting—Recommendations

6.B.1 The FIRM SHOULD present both POOLED FUND GROSS RETURNS and POOLED FUND NET RETURNS.

6.B.2 The FIRM SHOULD present the following items:

a. Cumulative returns of the POOLED FUND and the BENCHMARK for all periods.

b. Quarterly and/or monthly returns.

c. Annualized POOLED FUND and BENCHMARK returns for periods longer than 12 months.

6.B.3 For all periods for which an annualized EX POST STANDARD DEVIATION of the POOLED FUND and the BENCHMARK are presented, the FIRM SHOULD present the corresponding annualized return of the POOLED FUND and the BENCHMARK.

6.B.4 For all periods greater than three years for which an annualized return of the POOLED FUND and the BENCHMARK are presented, the FIRM SHOULD present the corresponding annualized EX POST STANDARD DEVIATION (using monthly returns) of the POOLED FUND and the BENCHMARK.

6.B.5 The FIRM SHOULD present relevant EX POST ADDITIONAL RISK MEASURES for the POOLED FUND and the BENCHMARK.

  

6.B.6 The FIRM SHOULD present more than 10 years of annual performance in the GIPS POOLED FUND REPORT.

6.B.7 The FIRM SHOULD present PROPRIETARY ASSETS as a percentage of POOLED FUND assets as of each annual period end.

6.B.8 If the FIRM uses preliminary, estimated values as FAIR VALUE, the FIRM SHOULD present the percentage of assets in the POOLED FUND that were valued using preliminary, estimated values as of each annual period end.

6.B.9 For REAL ESTATE POOLED FUNDS, the FIRM SHOULD present POOLED FUND and BENCHMARK COMPONENT RETURNS for all periods presented.

6.B.10 For POOLED FUNDS OF FUNDS, the FIRM SHOULD present the percentage, if any, of POOLED FUND assets that is invested in DIRECT INVESTMENTS (rather than in fund investment vehicles) as of each annual period end.

6.B.11 If the FIRM has COMMITTED CAPITAL, the FIRM SHOULD present FIRM-wide uncalled COMMITTED CAPITAL as of each annual period end.

6.B.12 The FIRM SHOULD present the total FAIR VALUE of the FIRM'S co-investments related to the POOLED FUND as of each annual period end.

## 6.C. Disclosure—Requirements

6.C.1 Once the FIRM has met all the applicable REQUIREMENTS of the GIPS standards, the FIRM MUST disclose its compliance with the GIPS standards using one of the following compliance statements. The compliance statement for a POOLED FUND MUST only be used in a GIPS POOLED FUND REPORT.

a. For a FIRM that is verified:

"[Insert name of FIRM] claims compliance with the Global Investment Performance Standards (GIPS®) and has prepared and presented this report in compliance with the GIPS standards. [Insert name of FIRM] has been independently verified for the periods [insert dates]. The verification report(s) is/are available upon request.

"A firm that claims compliance with the GIPS standards must establish policies and procedures for complying with all the applicable requirements of the GIPS standards. Verification provides assurance on whether the firm's policies and procedures related to composite and pooled fund maintenance, as well as the calculation, presentation, and distribution of performance, have been designed in compliance with the GIPS standards and have been implemented on a firm-wide basis. Verification does not provide assurance on the accuracy of any specific performance report."

  

b. For POOLED FUNDS of a verified FIRM that have also had a PERFORMANCE EXAMINATION:

> "[Insert name of FIRM] claims compliance with the Global Investment Performance Standards (GIPS®) and has prepared and presented this report in compliance with the GIPS standards. [Insert name of FIRM] has been independently verified for the periods [insert dates].
>
> "A firm that claims compliance with the GIPS standards must establish policies and procedures for complying with all the applicable requirements of the GIPS standards. Verification provides assurance on whether the firm's policies and procedures related to composite and pooled fund maintenance, as well as the calculation, presentation, and distribution of performance, have been designed in compliance with the GIPS standards and have been implemented on a firm-wide basis. The [insert name of POOLED FUND] has had a performance examination for the periods [insert dates]. The verification and performance examination reports are available upon request."

The compliance statement for a FIRM that is verified or for POOLED FUNDS of a verified FIRM that have also had a PERFORMANCE EXAMINATION is complete only when both paragraphs are shown together, one after the other.

c. For a FIRM that has not been verified:

> "[Insert name of FIRM] claims compliance with the Global Investment Performance Standards (GIPS®) and has prepared and presented this report in compliance with the GIPS standards. [Insert name of FIRM] has not been independently verified."

The FIRM MUST NOT exclude any portion of the respective compliance statement. Any modifications to the compliance statement MUST be additive.

**6.C.2** The FIRM MUST disclose the following: "GIPS® is a registered trademark of CFA Institute. CFA Institute does not endorse or promote this organization, nor does it warrant the accuracy or quality of the content contained herein."

**6.C.3** The FIRM MUST disclose the definition of the FIRM used to determine TOTAL FIRM ASSETS and FIRM-wide compliance.

**6.C.4** The FIRM MUST disclose the POOLED FUND DESCRIPTION.

**6.C.5** The FIRM MUST disclose:

a. The BENCHMARK DESCRIPTION, which MUST include the key features of the BENCHMARK or the name of the BENCHMARK for a readily recognized index or other point of reference.

b. The PERIODICITY of the BENCHMARK if BENCHMARK returns are calculated less frequently than monthly.

  

6.C.6 When presenting POOLED FUND GROSS RETURNS, the FIRM MUST disclose if any other fees are deducted in addition to TRANSACTION COSTS.

6.C.7 When presenting POOLED FUND NET RETURNS, the FIRM MUST disclose:

a. If POOLED FUND NET RETURNS are calculated using model or actual TOTAL POOLED FUND FEES.

b. If POOLED FUND NET RETURNS are net of any PERFORMANCE-BASED FEES or CARRIED INTEREST.

c. If model INVESTMENT MANAGEMENT FEES or model TOTAL POOLED FUND FEES are used and POOLED FUND GROSS RETURNS are not presented, the model INVESTMENT MANAGEMENT FEE or model TOTAL POOLED FUND FEE used to calculate POOLED FUND NET RETURNS.[48]

d. If model INVESTMENT MANAGEMENT FEES or model TOTAL POOLED FUND FEES are used, the methodology used to calculate POOLED FUND NET RETURNS.

e. If the POOLED FUND has a partnership structure, on which assets the POOLED FUND NET RETURNS are calculated.

f. If the POOLED FUND has multiple share classes, and one share class is used to calculate POOLED FUND NET RETURNS, the share class used to calculate POOLED FUND NET RETURNS.

6.C.8 The FIRM MUST disclose which fees and expenses other than INVESTMENT MANAGEMENT FEES (e.g., research costs) are separately charged by the FIRM to investors, if material.

6.C.9 The FIRM MUST disclose or otherwise indicate the reporting currency.

6.C.10 The FIRM MUST disclose the current FEE SCHEDULE appropriate to PROSPECTIVE INVESTORS.

6.C.11 If the FEE SCHEDULE includes PERFORMANCE-BASED FEES or CARRIED INTEREST, the FIRM MUST disclose the PERFORMANCE-BASED FEE DESCRIPTION or CARRIED INTEREST DESCRIPTION.

6.C.12 The FIRM MUST disclose the POOLED FUND INCEPTION DATE and what the POOLED FUND INCEPTION DATE represents.

6.C.13 The FIRM MUST disclose that the following lists are available upon request, if applicable:

a. List of COMPOSITE DESCRIPTIONS.

b. List of POOLED FUND DESCRIPTIONS for LIMITED DISTRIBUTION POOLED FUNDS.

c. List of BROAD DISTRIBUTION POOLED FUNDS.

6.C.14 The FIRM MUST disclose that policies for valuing investments, calculating performance, and preparing GIPS REPORTS are available upon request.

6.C.15 The FIRM MUST disclose how leverage, derivatives, and short positions have been used historically, if material.

[48] REQUIRED for periods ending on or after 31 December 2020.

**6.C.16** The FIRM MUST disclose all significant events that would help a PROSPECTIVE INVESTOR interpret the GIPS POOLED FUND REPORT. This disclosure MUST be included for a minimum of one year and for as long as it is relevant to interpreting the track record.

**6.C.17** For any performance presented for periods prior to the MINIMUM EFFECTIVE COMPLIANCE DATE that does not comply with the GIPS standards, the FIRM MUST disclose the periods of non-compliance.

**6.C.18** If the FIRM is redefined, the FIRM MUST disclose the date and description of the redefinition.

**6.C.19** If the POOLED FUND'S investment mandate, objective, or strategy is changed, the FIRM MUST disclose the date and description of the change.

**6.C.20** The FIRM MUST disclose changes to the name of the POOLED FUND. This disclosure MUST be included for a minimum of one year and for as long as it is relevant to interpreting the track record.

**6.C.21** The FIRM MUST disclose if POOLED FUND returns are gross or net of withholding taxes, if material.

**6.C.22** The FIRM MUST disclose if BENCHMARK returns are net of withholding taxes if this information is available.

**6.C.23** If the GIPS POOLED FUND REPORT conforms with laws and/or regulations that conflict with the REQUIREMENTS of the GIPS standards, the FIRM MUST disclose this fact and disclose the manner in which the laws and/or regulations conflict with the GIPS standards.

**6.C.24** The FIRM MUST disclose the use of a SUB-ADVISOR and the periods a SUB-ADVISOR was used.[49]

**6.C.25** The FIRM MUST disclose if the POOLED FUND'S valuation hierarchy materially differs from the RECOMMENDED valuation hierarchy. (See provision 2.B.6 for the RECOMMENDED valuation hierarchy.)[50]

**6.C.26** If the FIRM determines no appropriate BENCHMARK for the POOLED FUND exists, the FIRM MUST disclose why no BENCHMARK is presented.

**6.C.27** If the FIRM changes the BENCHMARK, the FIRM MUST disclose:

- **a.** For a prospective BENCHMARK change, the date and description of the change. Changes MUST be disclosed for as long as returns for the prior BENCHMARK are included in the GIPS POOLED FUND REPORT.
- **b.** For a retroactive BENCHMARK change, the date and description of the change. Changes MUST be disclosed for a minimum of one year and for as long as they are relevant to interpreting the track record.

[49] REQUIRED for periods beginning on or after 1 January 2006.

[50] REQUIRED for periods beginning on or after 1 January 2011.

  

**6.C.28** If a custom BENCHMARK or combination of multiple BENCHMARKS is used, the FIRM MUST:

a. Disclose the BENCHMARK components, weights, and rebalancing process, if applicable.

b. Disclose the calculation methodology.

c. Clearly label the BENCHMARK to indicate that it is a custom BENCHMARK.

**6.C.29** For POOLED FUNDS with at least three annual periods of performance, the FIRM MUST disclose if the three-year annualized EX POST STANDARD DEVIATION of the POOLED FUND and/or BENCHMARK is not presented because 36 monthly returns are not available.

**6.C.30** The FIRM MUST disclose if performance from a past firm or affiliation is presented and for which periods.

**6.C.31** The FIRM MUST disclose any change to the GIPS POOLED FUND REPORT resulting from the correction of a MATERIAL ERROR. Following the correction of the GIPS POOLED FUND REPORT, this disclosure MUST be included for a minimum of one year and for as long as it is relevant to interpreting the track record. This disclosure is not REQUIRED to be included in a GIPS POOLED FUND REPORT that is provided to a PROSPECTIVE INVESTOR that did not receive the GIPS POOLED FUND REPORT containing the MATERIAL ERROR.

**6.C.32** The FIRM MUST disclose if preliminary, estimated values are used to determine FAIR VALUE.

**6.C.33** If the FIRM changes the type of return(s) presented for the POOLED FUND (e.g., changes from MONEY-WEIGHTED RETURNS to TIME-WEIGHTED RETURNS), the FIRM MUST disclose the change and the date of the change. This disclosure MUST be included for a minimum of one year and for as long as it is relevant to interpreting the track record.

**6.C.34** If the FIRM presents ADDITIONAL RISK MEASURES, the FIRM MUST:

a. Describe any ADDITIONAL RISK MEASURE.

b. Disclose the name of the risk-free rate if a risk-free rate is used in the calculation of the ADDITIONAL RISK MEASURE.

**6.C.35** The FIRM MUST disclose if POOLED FUND GROSS RETURNS or POOLED FUND NET RETURNS are used to calculate presented risk measures.

**6.C.36** For REAL ESTATE investments that are not in a REAL ESTATE OPEN-END FUND, the FIRM MUST disclose that:[51]

a. EXTERNAL VALUATIONS are obtained, and the frequency with which they are obtained, or

b. The FIRM relies on valuations from financial statement audits.

**6.C.37** When the GIPS POOLED FUND REPORT includes THEORETICAL PERFORMANCE as SUPPLEMENTAL INFORMATION, the FIRM MUST:

a. Disclose that the results are theoretical, are not based on the performance of actual assets, and if the THEORETICAL PERFORMANCE was derived from the retroactive or prospective application of a model.

---

[51] REQUIRED for periods ending on or after 31 December 2020.

  

b. Disclose a basic description of the methodology and assumptions used to calculate the THEORETICAL PERFORMANCE sufficient for the PROSPECTIVE INVESTOR to interpret the THEORETICAL PERFORMANCE, including if it is based on model performance, backtested performance, or hypothetical performance.

c. Disclose whether the THEORETICAL PERFORMANCE reflects the deduction of actual or estimated INVESTMENT MANAGEMENT FEES, TRANSACTION COSTS, or other fees and charges that an actual POOLED FUND investor would have paid or will pay.

d. Clearly label the THEORETICAL PERFORMANCE as SUPPLEMENTAL INFORMATION.

## 6.D. Disclosure—Recommendations

6.D.1 The FIRM SHOULD disclose material changes to valuation policies and/or methodologies.

6.D.2 The FIRM SHOULD disclose material changes to calculation policies and/or methodologies.

6.D.3 The FIRM SHOULD disclose material differences between the BENCHMARK and the POOLED FUND'S investment mandate, objective, or strategy.

6.D.4 The FIRM SHOULD disclose the key assumptions used to value investments.

6.D.5 If a parent company contains multiple firms, each FIRM within the parent company SHOULD disclose a list of the other firms contained within the parent company.

6.D.6 If the FIRM adheres to any industry valuation guidelines in addition to the GIPS valuation REQUIREMENTS, the FIRM SHOULD disclose which guidelines have been applied.

6.D.7 When using BENCHMARKS that have limitations, such as peer group BENCHMARKS, the FIRM SHOULD disclose these limitations.

6.D.8 The FIRM SHOULD disclose how research costs are reflected in returns.

  

# 7. POOLED FUND MONEY-WEIGHTED RETURN REPORT

**The following provisions apply to POOLED FUNDS that include MONEY-WEIGHTED RETURNS in a GIPS POOLED FUND REPORT when the FIRM meets the REQUIREMENTS specified in provision 1.A.35 and chooses to present MONEY-WEIGHTED RETURNS.**

## 7.A. Presentation and Reporting—Requirements

7.A.1 The FIRM MUST present in each GIPS POOLED FUND REPORT:

a. The annualized POOLED FUND SINCE-INCEPTION MONEY-WEIGHTED RETURN through the most recent annual period end.

b. When the POOLED FUND has a track record that is less than a full year, the non-annualized POOLED FUND SINCE-INCEPTION MONEY-WEIGHTED RETURN through the initial annual period end.

c. When the POOLED FUND terminates, the annualized POOLED FUND SINCE-INCEPTION MONEY-WEIGHTED RETURN through the POOLED FUND TERMINATION DATE.

d. The SINCE-INCEPTION MONEY-WEIGHTED RETURN for the BENCHMARK for the same periods as presented for the POOLED FUND, unless the FIRM determines there is no appropriate BENCHMARK.

e. POOLED FUND assets as of the most recent annual period end.

f. TOTAL FIRM ASSETS as of the most recent annual period end.[52]

7.A.2 If a SUBSCRIPTION LINE OF CREDIT is used, the FIRM MUST present the POOLED FUND SINCE-INCEPTION MONEY-WEIGHTED RETURN both with and without the SUBSCRIPTION LINE OF CREDIT through the most recent annual period end. The FIRM is not REQUIRED to present returns without the SUBSCRIPTION LINE OF CREDIT when the SUBSCRIPTION LINE OF CREDIT has all of the following characteristics.[53]

a. The principal was repaid within 120 days using COMMITTED CAPITAL drawn down through a capital call.

b. No principal was used to fund DISTRIBUTIONS.

---

[52] REQUIRED for periods ending on or after 31 December 2020. For periods ending prior to 31 December 2020, FIRMS may present either TOTAL FIRM ASSETS or POOLED FUND assets as a percentage of TOTAL FIRM ASSETS.

[53] REQUIRED for periods ending on or after 31 December 2020.

**7.A.3** The FIRM MUST present the percentage of the total FAIR VALUE OF POOLED FUND assets that were valued using subjective unobservable inputs (as described in provision 2.B.6.e) as of the most recent annual period end, if such investments represent a material amount of POOLED FUND assets.

**7.A.4** If the POOLED FUND has COMMITTED CAPITAL, the FIRM MUST present the following items as of the most recent annual period end:

a. POOLED FUND SINCE-INCEPTION PAID-IN CAPITAL.

b. POOLED FUND SINCE-INCEPTION DISTRIBUTIONS.

c. POOLED FUND cumulative COMMITTED CAPITAL.

d. TOTAL VALUE to SINCE-INCEPTION PAID-IN CAPITAL (INVESTMENT MULTIPLE or TVPI).

e. SINCE-INCEPTION DISTRIBUTIONS to SINCE-INCEPTION PAID-IN CAPITAL (REALIZATION MULTIPLE or DPI).

f. SINCE-INCEPTION PAID-IN CAPITAL to cumulative COMMITTED CAPITAL (PIC MULTIPLE).

g. RESIDUAL VALUE to SINCE-INCEPTION PAID-IN CAPITAL (UNREALIZED MULTIPLE or RVPI).

**7.A.5** The FIRM MUST clearly label or identify:

a. The periods that are presented.

b. If POOLED FUND returns are POOLED FUND GROSS RETURNS or POOLED FUND NET RETURNS.

c. If POOLED FUND returns do or do not reflect the SUBSCRIPTION LINE OF CREDIT. This information is REQUIRED only if the FIRM presents returns both with and without the SUBSCRIPTION LINE OF CREDIT.

**7.A.6** If the FIRM includes more than one BENCHMARK in the GIPS POOLED FUND REPORT, the FIRM MUST present and disclose all REQUIRED information for all BENCHMARKS presented.

**7.A.7** The FIRM MUST present the POOLED FUND EXPENSE RATIO appropriate to PROSPECTIVE INVESTORS.

**7.A.8** If the FIRM chooses to present POOLED FUND uncalled COMMITTED CAPITAL or a combination of POOLED FUND assets and POOLED FUND uncalled COMMITTED CAPITAL, the FIRM MUST:

a. Present POOLED FUND uncalled COMMITTED CAPITAL for the same periods for which the combination of POOLED FUND assets and POOLED FUND uncalled COMMITTED CAPITAL is presented.

b. Clearly label POOLED FUND uncalled COMMITTED CAPITAL as such.

c. Clearly label the combination of POOLED FUND assets and POOLED FUND uncalled COMMITTED CAPITAL as such.

  

7.A.9 If the FIRM chooses to present FIRM-wide uncalled COMMITTED CAPITAL or a combination of TOTAL FIRM ASSETS and FIRM-wide uncalled COMMITTED CAPITAL, the FIRM MUST:

a. Present FIRM-wide uncalled COMMITTED CAPITAL for the same periods for which the combination of TOTAL FIRM ASSETS and FIRM-wide uncalled COMMITTED CAPITAL is presented.

b. Clearly label FIRM-wide uncalled COMMITTED CAPITAL as such.

c. Clearly label the combination of TOTAL FIRM ASSETS and FIRM-wide uncalled COMMITTED CAPITAL as such.

7.A.10 If the FIRM chooses to present ADVISORY-ONLY ASSETS that reflect the POOLED FUND'S investment mandate, objective, or strategy or a combination of POOLED FUND assets and ADVISORY-ONLY ASSETS that reflect the POOLED FUND'S investment mandate, objective, or strategy, the FIRM MUST:

a. Present ADVISORY-ONLY ASSETS that reflect the POOLED FUND'S investment mandate, objective, or strategy for the same periods for which the combination of POOLED FUND assets and ADVISORY-ONLY ASSETS that reflect the POOLED FUND'S investment mandate, objective, or strategy is presented.

b. Clearly label ADVISORY-ONLY ASSETS that reflect the POOLED FUND'S investment mandate, objective, or strategy as such.

c. Clearly label the combination of POOLED FUND assets and ADVISORY-ONLY ASSETS that reflect the POOLED FUND'S investment mandate, objective, or strategy as such.

7.A.11 If the FIRM chooses to present FIRM-wide ADVISORY-ONLY ASSETS or a combination of TOTAL FIRM ASSETS and FIRM-wide ADVISORY-ONLY ASSETS, the FIRM MUST:

a. Present FIRM-wide ADVISORY-ONLY ASSETS for the same periods for which the combination of TOTAL FIRM ASSETS and FIRM-wide ADVISORY-ONLY ASSETS is presented.

b. Clearly label FIRM-wide ADVISORY-ONLY ASSETS as such.

c. Clearly label the combination of TOTAL FIRM ASSETS and FIRM-wide ADVISORY-ONLY ASSETS as such.

7.A.12 All REQUIRED and RECOMMENDED information in the GIPS POOLED FUND REPORT MUST be presented in the same currency.

7.A.13 Any SUPPLEMENTAL INFORMATION included in the GIPS POOLED FUND REPORT:

a. MUST relate directly to the POOLED FUND.

b. MUST NOT contradict or conflict with the REQUIRED or RECOMMENDED information in the GIPS POOLED FUND REPORT.

c. MUST be clearly labeled as SUPPLEMENTAL INFORMATION.

## 7.B. Presentation and Reporting—Recommendations

7.B.1 The FIRM SHOULD present annualized SINCE-INCEPTION MONEY-WEIGHTED POOLED FUND GROSS RETURNS and SINCE-INCEPTION MONEY-WEIGHTED POOLED FUND NET RETURNS as of each annual period end.

7.B.2 If the POOLED FUND has COMMITTED CAPITAL, the FIRM SHOULD present the following items as of each annual period end:

a. POOLED FUND SINCE-INCEPTION PAID-IN CAPITAL.

b. POOLED FUND SINCE-INCEPTION DISTRIBUTIONS.

c. POOLED FUND cumulative COMMITTED CAPITAL.

d. TOTAL VALUE to SINCE-INCEPTION PAID-IN CAPITAL (INVESTMENT MULTIPLE or TVPI).

e. SINCE-INCEPTION DISTRIBUTIONS to SINCE-INCEPTION PAID-IN CAPITAL (REALIZATION MULTIPLE or DPI).

f. SINCE-INCEPTION PAID-IN CAPITAL to cumulative COMMITTED CAPITAL (PIC MULTIPLE).

g. RESIDUAL VALUE to SINCE-INCEPTION PAID-IN CAPITAL (UNREALIZED MULTIPLE or RVPI).

7.B.3 The FIRM SHOULD present PROPRIETARY ASSETS as a percentage of POOLED FUND assets as of the most recent annual period end.

7.B.4 The FIRM SHOULD present an appropriate EX POST risk measure for the POOLED FUND and the BENCHMARK. The same EX POST risk measure SHOULD be presented for the POOLED FUND and the BENCHMARK.

7.B.5 If the FIRM uses preliminary, estimated values as FAIR VALUE, the FIRM SHOULD present the percentage of assets in the POOLED FUND that were valued using preliminary, estimated values as of the most recent annual period end.

7.B.6 For POOLED FUNDS OF FUNDS, the FIRM SHOULD present the percentage, if any, of POOLED FUND assets that is invested in DIRECT INVESTMENTS (rather than in fund investment vehicles) as of the most recent annual period end.

7.B.7 If the FIRM has COMMITTED CAPITAL, the FIRM SHOULD present FIRM-wide uncalled COMMITTED CAPITAL as of the most recent annual period end.

7.B.8 The FIRM SHOULD present the total FAIR VALUE of the FIRM's co-investments related to the POOLED FUND as of the most recent annual period end.

  

## 7.C. Disclosure—Requirements

7.C.1 Once the FIRM has met all the applicable REQUIREMENTS of the GIPS standards, the FIRM MUST disclose its compliance with the GIPS standards using one of the following compliance statements. The compliance statement for a POOLED FUND MUST only be used in a GIPS POOLED FUND REPORT.

a. For a FIRM that is verified:

> "[Insert name of FIRM] claims compliance with the Global Investment Performance Standards (GIPS®) and has prepared and presented this report in compliance with the GIPS standards. [Insert name of FIRM] has been independently verified for the periods [insert dates]. The verification report(s) is/are available upon request.
>
> "A firm that claims compliance with the GIPS standards must establish policies and procedures for complying with all the applicable requirements of the GIPS standards. Verification provides assurance on whether the firm's policies and procedures related to composite and pooled fund maintenance, as well as the calculation, presentation, and distribution of performance, have been designed in compliance with the GIPS standards and have been implemented on a firm-wide basis. Verification does not provide assurance on the accuracy of any specific performance report."

b. For POOLED FUNDS of a verified FIRM that have also had a PERFORMANCE EXAMINATION:

> "[Insert name of FIRM] claims compliance with the Global Investment Performance Standards (GIPS®) and has prepared and presented this report in compliance with the GIPS standards. [Insert name of FIRM] has been independently verified for the periods [insert dates].
>
> "A firm that claims compliance with the GIPS standards must establish policies and procedures for complying with all the applicable requirements of the GIPS standards. Verification provides assurance on whether the firm's policies and procedures related to composite and pooled fund maintenance, as well as the calculation, presentation, and distribution of performance, have been designed in compliance with the GIPS standards and have been implemented on a firm-wide basis. The [insert name of POOLED FUND] has had a performance examination for the periods [insert dates]. The verification and performance examination reports are available upon request."

The compliance statement for a FIRM that is verified or for POOLED FUNDS of a verified FIRM that have also had a PERFORMANCE EXAMINATION is complete only when both paragraphs are shown together, one after the other.

c. For a FIRM that has not been verified:

"[Insert name of FIRM] claims compliance with the Global Investment Performance Standards (GIPS®) and has prepared and presented this report in compliance with the GIPS standards. [Insert name of FIRM] has not been independently verified."

The FIRM MUST NOT exclude any portion of the respective compliance statement. Any modifications to the compliance statement MUST be additive.

7.C.2 The FIRM MUST disclose the following: "GIPS® is a registered trademark of CFA Institute. CFA Institute does not endorse or promote this organization, nor does it warrant the accuracy or quality of the content contained herein."

7.C.3 The FIRM MUST disclose the definition of the FIRM used to determine TOTAL FIRM ASSETS and FIRM-wide compliance.

7.C.4 The FIRM MUST disclose the POOLED FUND DESCRIPTION.

7.C.5 The FIRM MUST disclose the BENCHMARK DESCRIPTION, which MUST include the key features of the BENCHMARK or the name of the BENCHMARK for a readily recognized index or other point of reference.

7.C.6 When presenting POOLED FUND GROSS RETURNS, the FIRM MUST disclose if any other fees are deducted in addition to TRANSACTION COSTS.

7.C.7 When presenting POOLED FUND NET RETURNS, the FIRM MUST disclose:

a. If POOLED FUND NET RETURNS are calculated using model or actual TOTAL POOLED FUND FEES.

b. If POOLED FUND NET RETURNS are net of any PERFORMANCE-BASED FEES or CARRIED INTEREST.

c. If model INVESTMENT MANAGEMENT FEES or model TOTAL POOLED FUND FEES are used and POOLED FUND GROSS RETURNS are not presented, the model INVESTMENT MANAGEMENT FEE or model TOTAL POOLED FUND FEE used to calculate POOLED FUND NET RETURNS.[54]

d. If model INVESTMENT MANAGEMENT FEES or model TOTAL POOLED FUND FEES are used, the methodology used to calculate POOLED FUND NET RETURNS.

e. If the POOLED FUND has a partnership structure, on which assets the POOLED FUND NET RETURNS are calculated.

f. If the POOLED FUND has multiple share classes, and one share class is used to calculate POOLED FUND NET RETURNS, the share class used to calculate POOLED FUND NET RETURNS.

7.C.8 The FIRM MUST disclose which fees and expenses other than INVESTMENT MANAGEMENT FEES (e.g., research costs) are separately charged by the FIRM to investors, if material.

[54] REQUIRED for periods ending on or after 31 December 2020.

  

7.C.9 The FIRM MUST disclose or otherwise indicate the reporting currency.

7.C.10 The FIRM MUST disclose the current FEE SCHEDULE appropriate to PROSPECTIVE INVESTORS.

7.C.11 If the FEE SCHEDULE includes PERFORMANCE-BASED FEES or CARRIED INTEREST, the FIRM MUST disclose the PERFORMANCE-BASED FEE DESCRIPTION or CARRIED INTEREST DESCRIPTION.

7.C.12 The FIRM MUST disclose the POOLED FUND INCEPTION DATE and what the POOLED FUND INCEPTION DATE represents.

7.C.13 The FIRM MUST disclose that the following lists are available upon request, if applicable:

a. List of COMPOSITE DESCRIPTIONS.

b. List of POOLED FUND DESCRIPTIONS for LIMITED DISTRIBUTION POOLED FUNDS.

c. List of BROAD DISTRIBUTION POOLED FUNDS.

7.C.14 The FIRM MUST disclose that policies for valuing investments, calculating performance, and preparing GIPS REPORTS are available upon request.

7.C.15 The FIRM MUST disclose how leverage, derivatives, and short positions have been used historically, if material.

7.C.16 The FIRM MUST disclose all significant events that would help a PROSPECTIVE INVESTOR interpret the GIPS POOLED FUND REPORT. This disclosure MUST be included for a minimum of one year and for as long as it is relevant to interpreting the track record.

7.C.17 For any performance presented for periods prior to the MINIMUM EFFECTIVE COMPLIANCE DATE that does not comply with the GIPS standards, the FIRM MUST disclose the periods of non-compliance.

7.C.18 If the FIRM is redefined, the FIRM MUST disclose the date and description of the redefinition.

7.C.19 If the POOLED FUND'S investment mandate, objective, or strategy is changed, the FIRM MUST disclose the date and description of the change.

7.C.20 The FIRM MUST disclose changes to the name of the POOLED FUND. This disclosure MUST be included for a minimum of one year and for as long as it is relevant to interpreting the track record.

7.C.21 The FIRM MUST disclose if POOLED FUND returns are gross or net of withholding taxes, if material.

7.C.22 The FIRM MUST disclose if BENCHMARK returns are net of withholding taxes if this information is available.

7.C.23 If the GIPS POOLED FUND REPORT conforms with laws and/or regulations that conflict with the REQUIREMENTS of the GIPS standards, the FIRM MUST disclose this fact and disclose the manner in which the laws and/or regulations conflict with the GIPS standards.

  

**7.C.24** The FIRM MUST disclose the use of a SUB-ADVISOR and the periods a SUB-ADVISOR was used.[55]

**7.C.25** The FIRM MUST disclose if the POOLED FUND'S valuation hierarchy materially differs from the RECOMMENDED valuation hierarchy.[56] (See provision 2.B.6 for the RECOMMENDED valuation hierarchy.)

**7.C.26** If the FIRM determines no appropriate BENCHMARK for the POOLED FUND exists, the FIRM MUST disclose why no BENCHMARK is presented.

**7.C.27** If the FIRM changes the BENCHMARK, the FIRM MUST disclose:

a. For a prospective BENCHMARK change, the date and description of the change. Changes MUST be disclosed for as long as returns for the prior BENCHMARK are included in the GIPS POOLED FUND REPORT.

b. For a retroactive BENCHMARK change, the date and description of the change. Changes MUST be disclosed for a minimum of one year and for as long as it is relevant to interpreting the track record.

**7.C.28** If a custom BENCHMARK or combination of multiple BENCHMARKS is used, the FIRM MUST:

a. Disclose the BENCHMARK components, weights, and rebalancing process, if applicable.

b. Disclose the calculation methodology.

c. Clearly label the BENCHMARK to indicate that it is a custom BENCHMARK.

**7.C.29** The FIRM MUST disclose the calculation methodology used for the BENCHMARK. If the FIRM presents the PUBLIC MARKET EQUIVALENT of a POOLED FUND as a BENCHMARK, the FIRM MUST also disclose the index used to calculate the PUBLIC MARKET EQUIVALENT.

**7.C.30** The FIRM MUST disclose if performance from a past firm or affiliation is presented and for which periods.

**7.C.31** The FIRM MUST disclose the frequency of EXTERNAL CASH FLOWS used in the MONEY-WEIGHTED RETURN calculation if daily frequency was not used.

**7.C.32** If a SUBSCRIPTION LINE OF CREDIT is used, and the FIRM is REQUIRED to present returns both with and without the SUBSCRIPTION LINE OF CREDIT, the FIRM MUST disclose:

a. The purpose for using the SUBSCRIPTION LINE OF CREDIT.

b. The size of the SUBSCRIPTION LINE OF CREDIT as of the most recent annual period end.

c. The SUBSCRIPTION LINE OF CREDIT amount outstanding as of the most recent annual period end.

---

[55] REQUIRED for periods beginning on or after 1 January 2006.

[56] REQUIRED for periods beginning on or after 1 January 2011.

  

**7.C.33** The FIRM MUST disclose any change to the GIPS POOLED FUND REPORT resulting from the correction of a MATERIAL ERROR. Following the correction of the GIPS POOLED FUND REPORT, this disclosure MUST be included for a minimum of one year and for as long as it is relevant to interpreting the track record. This disclosure is not REQUIRED to be included in a GIPS POOLED FUND REPORT that is provided to a PROSPECTIVE INVESTOR that did not receive the GIPS POOLED FUND REPORT containing the MATERIAL ERROR.

**7.C.34** The FIRM MUST disclose if preliminary, estimated values are used to determine FAIR VALUE.

**7.C.35** If the FIRM changes the type of return(s) presented for the POOLED FUND (e.g., changes from TIME-WEIGHTED RETURNS to MONEY-WEIGHTED RETURNS), the FIRM MUST disclose the change and the date of the change. This disclosure MUST be included for a minimum of one year and for as long as it is relevant to interpreting the track record.

**7.C.36** If the FIRM presents ADDITIONAL RISK MEASURES, the FIRM MUST:

a. Describe any ADDITIONAL RISK MEASURE.

b. Disclose the name of the risk-free rate if a risk-free rate is used in the calculation of the ADDITIONAL RISK MEASURE.

**7.C.37** The FIRM MUST disclose if POOLED FUND GROSS RETURNS or POOLED FUND NET RETURNS are used to calculate presented risk measures.

**7.C.38** For REAL ESTATE investments that are not in a REAL ESTATE OPEN-END FUND, the FIRM MUST disclose that:[57]

a. EXTERNAL VALUATIONS are obtained, and the frequency with which they are obtained, or

b. The FIRM relies on valuations from financial statement audits.

**7.C.39** When the GIPS POOLED FUND REPORT includes THEORETICAL PERFORMANCE as SUPPLEMENTAL INFORMATION, the FIRM MUST:

a. Disclose that the results are theoretical, are not based on the performance of actual assets, and if the THEORETICAL PERFORMANCE was derived from the retroactive or prospective application of a model.

b. Disclose a basic description of the methodology and assumptions used to calculate the THEORETICAL PERFORMANCE sufficient for the PROSPECTIVE INVESTOR to interpret the THEORETICAL PERFORMANCE, including if it is based on model performance, backtested performance, or hypothetical performance.

c. Disclose whether the THEORETICAL PERFORMANCE reflects the deduction of actual or estimated INVESTMENT MANAGEMENT FEES, TRANSACTION COSTS, or other fees and charges that an actual POOLED FUND investor would have paid or will pay.

d. Clearly label the THEORETICAL PERFORMANCE as SUPPLEMENTAL INFORMATION.

---

[57] REQUIRED for periods ending on or after 31 December 2020.

## 7.D. Disclosure—Recommendations

7.D.1 The FIRM SHOULD disclose material changes to valuation policies and/or methodologies.

7.D.2 The FIRM SHOULD disclose material changes to calculation policies and/or methodologies.

7.D.3 The FIRM SHOULD disclose material differences between the BENCHMARK and the POOLED FUND's investment mandate, objective, or strategy.

7.D.4 The FIRM SHOULD disclose the key assumptions used to value investments.

7.D.5 If a parent company contains multiple firms, each FIRM within the parent company SHOULD disclose a list of the other firms contained within the parent company.

7.D.6 If the FIRM adheres to any industry valuation guidelines in addition to the GIPS valuation REQUIREMENTS, the FIRM SHOULD disclose which guidelines have been applied.

7.D.7 When using BENCHMARKS that have limitations, such as peer group BENCHMARKS, the FIRM SHOULD disclose these limitations.

7.D.8 The FIRM SHOULD disclose how research costs are reflected in returns.

  

# 8. GIPS ADVERTISING GUIDELINES

## Purpose of the GIPS Advertising Guidelines

The GIPS Advertising Guidelines provide FIRMS with options for advertising when mentioning the FIRM'S claim of compliance. The GIPS Advertising Guidelines do not replace the GIPS standards, nor do they absolve FIRMS from presenting GIPS COMPOSITE REPORTS and GIPS POOLED FUND REPORTS as REQUIRED by the GIPS standards. These guidelines apply only to FIRMS that already satisfy all the applicable REQUIREMENTS of the GIPS standards on a FIRM-wide basis and prepare an advertisement that adheres to the REQUIREMENTS of the GIPS Advertising Guidelines (a "GIPS ADVERTISEMENT"). FIRMS may also choose to include a GIPS COMPOSITE REPORT or GIPS POOLED FUND REPORT in the advertisement.

## Definitions

### Advertisement

For the GIPS Advertising Guidelines, an advertisement includes any materials that are distributed to or designed for use in newspapers, magazines, FIRM brochures, POOLED FUND fact sheets, POOLED FUND offering documents, letters, media, websites, or any other written or electronic material distributed to more than one party, and there is no contact between the FIRM and the reader of the advertisement. One-on-one presentations and individual client reporting are not considered advertisements.

### GIPS Advertisement

A GIPS ADVERTISEMENT is an advertisement by a GIPS-compliant FIRM that adheres to the REQUIREMENTS of the GIPS Advertising Guidelines.

## Relationship of the GIPS Advertising Guidelines to Regulatory Requirements

When preparing GIPS ADVERTISEMENTS, FIRMS MUST also adhere to all applicable laws and regulations governing advertisements. FIRMS are encouraged to seek legal or regulatory counsel because additional disclosures may be REQUIRED. In cases where applicable laws or regulations conflict with the REQUIREMENTS of the GIPS standards or the GIPS Advertising Guidelines, FIRMS are REQUIRED to comply with the laws or regulations.

  

## Other Information

The GIPS ADVERTISEMENT may include other information beyond what is REQUIRED or RECOMMENDED under the GIPS Advertising Guidelines provided the information is shown with equal or lesser prominence relative to the information REQUIRED or RECOMMENDED by the GIPS Advertising Guidelines and the information does not conflict with the REQUIREMENTS or RECOMMENDATIONS of the GIPS standards or the GIPS Advertising Guidelines. FIRMS MUST adhere to the principles of fair representation and full disclosure when advertising and MUST NOT present performance or PERFORMANCE-RELATED INFORMATION that is false or misleading.

## 8.A. Fundamental Requirements of the GIPS Advertising Guidelines

**8.A.1** The GIPS Advertising Guidelines apply only to FIRMS that already claim compliance with the GIPS standards.

**8.A.2** A FIRM that chooses to claim compliance in a GIPS ADVERTISEMENT MUST comply with all applicable REQUIREMENTS of the GIPS Advertising Guidelines.

**8.A.3** The FIRM MUST maintain all data and information necessary to support all items included in a GIPS ADVERTISEMENT.

**8.A.4** Returns for periods of less than one year included in a GIPS ADVERTISEMENT MUST NOT be annualized.

**8.A.5** When TIME-WEIGHTED RETURNS are presented in a GIPS ADVERTISEMENT, the FIRM MUST NOT LINK non-GIPS-compliant performance for periods beginning on or after the MINIMUM EFFECTIVE COMPLIANCE DATE to GIPS-compliant performance. The FIRM may LINK non-GIPS-compliant performance to GIPS-compliant performance in a GIPS ADVERTISEMENT provided that only GIPS-compliant performance is presented for periods beginning on or after the MINIMUM EFFECTIVE COMPLIANCE DATE.

**8.A.6** When MONEY-WEIGHTED RETURNS are presented in a GIPS ADVERTISEMENT, the FIRM MUST NOT LINK non-GIPS-compliant performance for periods ending on or after the MINIMUM EFFECTIVE COMPLIANCE DATE to GIPS-compliant performance. The FIRM may LINK non-GIPS-compliant performance to GIPS-compliant performance in a GIPS ADVERTISEMENT provided that only GIPS-compliant performance is presented for periods ending on or after the MINIMUM EFFECTIVE COMPLIANCE DATE.

**8.A.7** COMPOSITE returns included in a GIPS ADVERTISEMENT MUST be derived from the returns included in or that will be included in the corresponding GIPS COMPOSITE REPORT.

**8.A.8** Disclosures included in a GIPS ADVERTISEMENT for a COMPOSITE MUST be consistent with the related disclosure included in the corresponding GIPS COMPOSITE REPORT, unless the disclosure included in the GIPS ADVERTISEMENT is more current and has not yet been reflected in the corresponding GIPS COMPOSITE REPORT.

8.A.9 LIMITED DISTRIBUTION POOLED FUND returns included in a GIPS ADVERTISEMENT MUST be derived from the returns included in or that will be included in the corresponding GIPS POOLED FUND REPORT.

8.A.10 Disclosures included in a GIPS ADVERTISEMENT for a LIMITED DISTRIBUTION POOLED FUND MUST be consistent with the related disclosure included in the corresponding GIPS POOLED FUND REPORT, unless the disclosure included in the GIPS ADVERTISEMENT is more current and has not yet been reflected in the corresponding GIPS POOLED FUND REPORT.

8.A.11 BENCHMARK returns included in a GIPS ADVERTISEMENT MUST be TOTAL RETURNS.

8.A.12 The FIRM MUST clearly label or identify:

a. The name of the COMPOSITE or POOLED FUND for which the GIPS ADVERTISEMENT is prepared.

b. The name of any BENCHMARK included in the GIPS ADVERTISEMENT.

c. The periods that are presented in the GIPS ADVERTISEMENT.

8.A.13 Other information beyond what is REQUIRED or RECOMMENDED under the GIPS Advertising Guidelines (e.g., COMPOSITE or POOLED FUND returns for additional periods) MUST be presented with equal or lesser prominence relative to the information REQUIRED or RECOMMENDED by the GIPS Advertising Guidelines. This information MUST NOT conflict with the REQUIREMENTS or RECOMMENDATIONS of the GIPS standards or the GIPS Advertising Guidelines.

8.A.14 All REQUIRED and RECOMMENDED information in a GIPS ADVERTISEMENT MUST be presented in the same currency.

## 8.B. GIPS Advertisements That Do Not Include Performance

8.B.1 The FIRM MUST disclose the GIPS Advertising Guidelines compliance statement:

> "[Insert name of FIRM] claims compliance with the Global Investment Performance Standards (GIPS®)."

8.B.2 The FIRM MUST disclose the following: "GIPS® is a registered trademark of CFA Institute. CFA Institute does not endorse or promote this organization, nor does it warrant the accuracy or quality of the content contained herein."

8.B.3 The FIRM MUST disclose how to obtain GIPS-compliant performance information for the FIRM's strategies and products.

  

# COMPOSITES

## 8.C. GIPS Advertisements for a Composite That Include Performance—Requirements

8.C.1 If TIME-WEIGHTED RETURNS are presented in the corresponding GIPS COMPOSITE REPORT, the FIRM MUST present COMPOSITE TOTAL RETURNS according to one of the following:

a. One-, three-, and five-year annualized COMPOSITE returns through the most recent period. If the COMPOSITE has been in existence for less than five years, the FIRM MUST also present the annualized return since the COMPOSITE INCEPTION DATE.

b. The period-to-date COMPOSITE return in addition to one-, three-, and five-year annualized COMPOSITE returns through the same period as presented in the corresponding GIPS COMPOSITE REPORT. If the COMPOSITE has been in existence for less than five years, the FIRM MUST also present the annualized return since the COMPOSITE INCEPTION DATE.

c. The period-to-date COMPOSITE return in addition to five years of annual COMPOSITE returns (or for each annual period since the COMPOSITE INCEPTION DATE if the COMPOSITE has been in existence for less than five years). The annual returns MUST be calculated through the same period as presented in the corresponding GIPS COMPOSITE REPORT.

d. The annualized COMPOSITE return for the total period that includes all periods presented in the corresponding GIPS COMPOSITE REPORT, through either:

   i. The most recent period end, or

   ii. The most recent annual period end.

8.C.2 If MONEY-WEIGHTED RETURNS are presented in the corresponding GIPS COMPOSITE REPORT, the FIRM MUST present the annualized (for periods longer than one year) or non-annualized (for periods less than one year) COMPOSITE SINCE-INCEPTION MONEY-WEIGHTED RETURN through either:

a. The most recent period end, or

b. The most recent annual period end.

8.C.3 The FIRM MUST clearly label COMPOSITE returns as GROSS-OF-FEES or NET-OF-FEES.

8.C.4 The FIRM MUST present BENCHMARK returns for the same BENCHMARK as presented in the corresponding GIPS COMPOSITE REPORT, if the corresponding GIPS COMPOSITE REPORT includes BENCHMARK returns. BENCHMARK returns MUST be of the same return type (TIME-WEIGHTED RETURNS or MONEY-WEIGHTED RETURNS), in the same currency, and for the same periods for which the COMPOSITE returns are presented.

  

8.C.5 The FIRM MUST disclose or otherwise indicate the reporting currency.

8.C.6 The FIRM MUST disclose the GIPS Advertising Guidelines compliance statement:

> "[Insert name of FIRM] claims compliance with the Global Investment Performance Standards (GIPS®)."

8.C.7 The FIRM MUST disclose the following: "GIPS® is a registered trademark of CFA Institute. CFA Institute does not endorse or promote this organization, nor does it warrant the accuracy or quality of the content contained herein."

8.C.8 The FIRM MUST disclose how to obtain a GIPS COMPOSITE REPORT.

8.C.9 The FIRM MUST disclose if the GIPS ADVERTISEMENT conforms with laws or regulations that conflict with the REQUIREMENTS or RECOMMENDATIONS of the GIPS standards or the GIPS Advertising Guidelines, as well as the manner in which the laws or regulations conflict with the GIPS standards or the GIPS Advertising Guidelines.

## 8.D. GIPS Advertisements for a Composite That Include Performance—Recommendations

8.D.1 The FIRM SHOULD disclose the COMPOSITE DESCRIPTION.

8.D.2 The FIRM SHOULD disclose how leverage, derivatives, and short positions have been used historically, if material.

8.D.3 The FIRM SHOULD disclose the BENCHMARK DESCRIPTION, which MUST include the key features of the BENCHMARK or the name of the BENCHMARK for a readily recognized index or other point of reference.

8.D.4 If the FIRM determines no appropriate BENCHMARK for the COMPOSITE exists, the FIRM SHOULD disclose why no BENCHMARK is presented.

8.D.5 The FIRM SHOULD disclose the definition of the FIRM.

# LIMITED DISTRIBUTION POOLED FUNDS

## 8.E. GIPS Advertisements for a Limited Distribution Pooled Fund That Include Performance—Requirements

8.E.1 If TIME-WEIGHTED RETURNS are presented in the corresponding GIPS REPORT, the FIRM MUST present TIME-WEIGHTED RETURNS for the POOLED FUND according to one of the following:

a. One-, three-, and five-year annualized returns through the most recent period. If the POOLED FUND has been in existence for less than five years, the FIRM MUST also present the annualized return since the POOLED FUND INCEPTION DATE.

b. The period-to-date return in addition to one-, three-, and five-year annualized returns through the same period as presented in the corresponding GIPS REPORT. If the POOLED FUND has been in existence for less than five years, the FIRM MUST also present the annualized return since the POOLED FUND INCEPTION DATE.

c. The period-to-date return in addition to five years of annual returns (or for each annual period since the POOLED FUND INCEPTION DATE if the POOLED FUND has been in existence for less than five years). The annual returns MUST be calculated through the same period as presented in the corresponding GIPS REPORT.

d. The annualized POOLED FUND return for the total period that includes all periods presented in the corresponding GIPS REPORT, through either:

   i. The most recent period end, or

   ii. The most recent annual period end.

8.E.2 If MONEY-WEIGHTED RETURNS are presented in the corresponding GIPS REPORT, the FIRM MUST present the annualized (for periods longer than one year) or non-annualized (for periods less than one year) SINCE-INCEPTION MONEY-WEIGHTED RETURN for the POOLED FUND through either:

a. The most recent period end, or

b. The most recent annual period end.

8.E.3 The FIRM MUST clearly label POOLED FUND returns as gross or net of TOTAL POOLED FUND FEES.

8.E.4 The FIRM MUST present BENCHMARK returns for the same BENCHMARK as presented in the corresponding GIPS REPORT, if the corresponding GIPS REPORT includes BENCHMARK returns. BENCHMARK returns MUST be of the same return type (TIME-WEIGHTED RETURNS or MONEY-WEIGHTED RETURNS), in the same currency, and for the same periods for which the POOLED FUND returns are presented.

8.E.5 The FIRM MUST disclose or otherwise indicate the reporting currency.

8.E.6 The FIRM MUST disclose the GIPS Advertising Guidelines compliance statement:

> "[Insert name of FIRM] claims compliance with the Global Investment Performance Standards (GIPS®)."

8.E.7 The FIRM MUST disclose the following: "GIPS® is a registered trademark of CFA Institute. CFA Institute does not endorse or promote this organization, nor does it warrant the accuracy or quality of the content contained herein."

8.E.8 The FIRM MUST disclose how to obtain a GIPS REPORT.

  

8.E.9 The FIRM MUST disclose if the GIPS ADVERTISEMENT conforms with laws or regulations that conflict with the REQUIREMENTS or RECOMMENDATIONS of the GIPS standards or the GIPS Advertising Guidelines, as well as the manner in which the laws or regulations conflict with the GIPS standards or the GIPS Advertising Guidelines.

## 8.F. GIPS Advertisements for a Limited Distribution Pooled Fund That Include Performance—Recommendations

8.F.1 The FIRM SHOULD disclose the POOLED FUND DESCRIPTION.

8.F.2 The FIRM SHOULD disclose how leverage, derivatives, and short positions have been used historically, if material.

8.F.3 The FIRM SHOULD disclose the BENCHMARK DESCRIPTION, which MUST include the key features of the BENCHMARK or the name of the BENCHMARK for a readily recognized index or other point of reference.

8.F.4 If the FIRM determines no appropriate BENCHMARK for the POOLED FUND exists, the FIRM SHOULD disclose why no BENCHMARK is presented.

8.F.5 The FIRM SHOULD disclose the definition of the FIRM.

# BROAD DISTRIBUTION POOLED FUNDS

## 8.G. GIPS Advertisements for a Broad Distribution Pooled Fund That Include Performance—Requirements

8.G.1 If laws or regulations mandate specific POOLED FUND returns, the FIRM MUST present POOLED FUND returns according to the methodology and for the periods REQUIRED by laws or regulations.

8.G.2 If specific periods are not mandated by laws or regulations, POOLED FUND returns MUST be presented consistent with one of the following options:

a. One-, three-, and five-year annualized returns through the most recent period. If the POOLED FUND has been in existence for less than five years, the FIRM MUST also present the annualized return since the POOLED FUND INCEPTION DATE.

b. The period-to-date return in addition to one-, three-, and five-year annualized returns through the most recent period. If the POOLED FUND has been in existence for less than five years, the FIRM MUST also present the annualized return since the POOLED FUND INCEPTION DATE.

c. The period-to-date return in addition to five years of annual returns (or for each annual period since the POOLED FUND INCEPTION DATE if the POOLED FUND has been in existence for less than five years).

d. The annualized POOLED FUND return since the POOLED FUND INCEPTION DATE through the most recent period.

8.G.3 If the GIPS ADVERTISEMENT is created for a specific POOLED FUND share class, and POOLED FUND NET RETURNS are presented, POOLED FUND NET RETURNS MUST reflect the fees and expenses of that specific share class.

8.G.4 If the GIPS ADVERTISEMENT is not created for a specific share class, and POOLED FUND NET RETURNS are presented, POOLED FUND NET RETURNS MUST reflect the fees and expenses of:

a. The share class with the maximum fee that is available for general distribution, or

b. All share classes.

8.G.5 The FIRM MUST clearly label POOLED FUND returns as gross or net of TOTAL POOLED FUND FEES.

8.G.6 The FIRM MUST present BENCHMARK TOTAL RETURNS for the same periods for which the POOLED FUND is presented, unless the FIRM determines there is no appropriate BENCHMARK.

8.G.7 The FIRM MUST disclose the current EXPENSE RATIO and which fees and expenses are included in the EXPENSE RATIO. The FIRM MUST disclose if PERFORMANCE-BASED FEES are not reflected in the EXPENSE RATIO, if applicable.

8.G.8 The FIRM MUST disclose or otherwise indicate the reporting currency.

8.G.9 The FIRM MUST disclose the POOLED FUND DESCRIPTION.

8.G.10 If laws or regulations mandate specific information about the POOLED FUND'S risk, as either a qualitative narrative or a quantitative metric, the FIRM MUST disclose this information.

8.G.11 If laws or regulations do not mandate specific information about the POOLED FUND'S risk, the FIRM MUST choose and present an appropriate risk measure or qualitative disclosure that a PROSPECTIVE INVESTOR is likely to understand.

8.G.12 The FIRM MUST disclose the BENCHMARK DESCRIPTION, which MUST include the key features of the BENCHMARK or the name of the BENCHMARK for a readily recognized index or other point of reference.

8.G.13 The FIRM MUST disclose the GIPS Advertising Guidelines compliance statement:

> "[Insert name of FIRM] claims compliance with the Global Investment Performance Standards (GIPS®)."

8.G.14 The FIRM MUST disclose the following: "GIPS® is a registered trademark of CFA Institute. CFA Institute does not endorse or promote this organization, nor does it warrant the accuracy or quality of the content contained herein."

 

8.G.15 The FIRM MUST disclose if the GIPS ADVERTISEMENT conforms with laws or regulations that conflict with the REQUIREMENTS or RECOMMENDATIONS of the GIPS standards or the GIPS Advertising Guidelines, as well as the manner in which the laws or regulations conflict with the GIPS standards or the GIPS Advertising Guidelines.

## 8.H. GIPS Advertisements for a Broad Distribution Pooled Fund That Include Performance—Recommendations

8.H.1 If the FIRM determines no appropriate BENCHMARK for the POOLED FUND exists, the FIRM SHOULD disclose why no BENCHMARK is presented.

8.H.2 The FIRM SHOULD disclose the POOLED FUND'S SALES CHARGES AND LOADS.

8.H.3 The FIRM SHOULD disclose how SALES CHARGES AND LOADS are reflected in the POOLED FUND'S returns, if applicable.

8.H.4 The FIRM SHOULD disclose the definition of the FIRM.



 

# GLOSSARY

**ACCRUAL ACCOUNTING** The recording of transactions as income is earned or expenses are incurred, rather than when income is received or expenses are paid (i.e., cash basis).

**ADDITIONAL RISK MEASURES** Risk measures included in a GIPS COMPOSITE REPORT or GIPS POOLED FUND REPORT beyond those REQUIRED to be presented.

**ADMINISTRATIVE FEE** All fees other than TRANSACTION COSTS and the INVESTMENT MANAGEMENT FEE. ADMINISTRATIVE FEES may include CUSTODY FEES, accounting fees, auditing fees, consulting fees, legal fees, performance measurement fees, and other related fees.

**ADVISORY-ONLY ASSETS** Assets for which the FIRM provides investment recommendations but has no control over implementation of investment decisions and no trading authority.

**ALL-IN FEE** A type of BUNDLED FEE that can include any combination of INVESTMENT MANAGEMENT FEES, TRANSACTION COSTS, CUSTODY FEES, and ADMINISTRATIVE FEES. ALL-IN FEES are typically offered in certain jurisdictions where asset management, brokerage, and custody services are offered by the same company.

**BENCHMARK** A point of reference against which the COMPOSITE'S or POOLED FUND'S returns or risk are compared.

**BENCHMARK DESCRIPTION** General information regarding the investments, structure, and characteristics of the BENCHMARK. The description MUST include the key features of the BENCHMARK or the name of the BENCHMARK for a readily recognized index or other point of reference.

**BROAD DISTRIBUTION POOLED FUND** A POOLED FUND that is regulated under a framework that would permit the general public to purchase or hold the POOLED FUND'S shares and is not exclusively offered in one-on-one presentations.

**BUNDLED FEE** A fee that combines multiple fees into one total or "bundled" fee. BUNDLED FEES can include any combination of INVESTMENT MANAGEMENT FEES, TRANSACTION COSTS, CUSTODY FEES, and/or ADMINISTRATIVE FEES. Two examples of BUNDLED FEES are WRAP FEES and ALL-IN FEES.

  

| | |
|---|---|
| **CAPITAL EMPLOYED** | The denominator of the COMPONENT RETURN calculation, defined as the "weighted-average equity" (weighted-average capital) during the measurement period. CAPITAL EMPLOYED does not include any INCOME RETURN or CAPITAL RETURN earned during the measurement period. Beginning capital is adjusted by weighting the EXTERNAL CASH FLOWS that occurred during the period. |
| **CAPITAL RETURN** | The change in value of the REAL ESTATE investments and cash and/or cash equivalent assets held throughout the measurement period, adjusted for all capital expenditures (subtracted) and net proceeds from sales (added). The CAPITAL RETURN is computed as a percentage of the CAPITAL EMPLOYED. Also known as "capital appreciation return" or "appreciation return." |
| **CARRIED INTEREST** | The profits that the GENERAL PARTNER is allocated from the profits on the investments made by the investment vehicle. Also known as "carry" or "promote." |
| **CARRIED INTEREST DESCRIPTION** | Information about the features of the CARRIED INTEREST calculation, such as the HURDLE RATE, CRYSTALLIZATION SCHEDULE, and HIGH WATERMARK. |
| **CARVE-OUT** | A portion of a PORTFOLIO that is by itself representative of a distinct investment strategy. It may be used to create a track record for a narrower mandate from a multiple-strategy PORTFOLIO managed to a broader mandate. |
| **CLAWBACK** | The repayment of previously earned PERFORMANCE-BASED FEES resulting from subsequent underperformance. |
| **CLOSED-END** | A POOLED FUND that is not open for subscriptions and/or redemptions. |
| **COMMITTED CAPITAL** | Pledges of capital to an investment vehicle by investors (LIMITED PARTNERS and the GENERAL PARTNER) or the FIRM. COMMITTED CAPITAL is typically drawn down over a period of time. Also known as "commitments." |
| **COMPONENT RETURNS** | The CAPITAL RETURNS and INCOME RETURNS of a REAL ESTATE COMPOSITE, REAL ESTATE POOLED FUND, or a BENCHMARK. |
| **COMPOSITE** | An aggregation of one or more PORTFOLIOS that are managed according to a similar investment mandate, objective, or strategy. |

*(continued)*

**COMPOSITE CREATION DATE** — The date when the FIRM first groups one or more PORTFOLIOS to create a COMPOSITE. The COMPOSITE CREATION DATE is not necessarily the same as the COMPOSITE INCEPTION DATE.

**COMPOSITE DEFINITION** — Detailed criteria that determine the assignment of PORTFOLIOS to COMPOSITES. Criteria may include, but are not limited to, investment mandate, style or strategy, asset class, the use of derivatives, leverage and/or hedging, targeted risk metrics, investment constraints or restrictions, and/or PORTFOLIO type (e.g., SEGREGATED ACCOUNT or POOLED FUND; taxable versus tax exempt).

**COMPOSITE DESCRIPTION** — General information regarding the investment mandate, objective, or strategy of the COMPOSITE. The COMPOSITE DESCRIPTION may be more abbreviated than the COMPOSITE DEFINITION but MUST include all key features of the COMPOSITE and MUST include enough information to allow a PROSPECTIVE CLIENT to understand the key characteristics of the COMPOSITE's investment mandate, objective, or strategy, including:

- The material risks of the COMPOSITE's strategy.
- How leverage, derivatives, and short positions may be used, if they are a material part of the strategy.
- If ILLIQUID INVESTMENTS are a material part of the strategy.

**COMPOSITE INCEPTION DATE** — The initial date of the COMPOSITE's track record.

**COMPOSITE TERMINATION DATE** — The date that the last PORTFOLIO exits a COMPOSITE, or the date that the FIRM no longer manages the strategy for SEGREGATED ACCOUNTS or offers the strategy to PROSPECTIVE CLIENTS.

**CRYSTALLIZATION SCHEDULE** — The point in time when the FIRM is entitled to receive the PERFORMANCE-BASED FEE and the fee is effectively earned.

**CUSTODY FEE** — The fee payable to the custodian for the safekeeping of PORTFOLIO assets. CUSTODY FEES are considered to be ADMINISTRATIVE FEES and typically contain an asset-based portion and a transaction-based portion. The CUSTODY FEE may also include charges for additional services, including accounting, securities lending, and/or performance measurement. Custodial fees that are charged per transaction SHOULD be included in the CUSTODY FEE and not included as part of TRANSACTION COSTS.

**DIRECT INVESTMENTS** — Investments made directly in companies rather than investments made in fund investment vehicles or cash and/or cash equivalents.

  

| | |
|---|---|
| **DISTINCT BUSINESS ENTITY** | A unit, division, department, or office that is organizationally and functionally segregated from other units, divisions, departments, or offices and that retains discretion over the assets it manages and that SHOULD have autonomy over the investment decision-making process. Possible criteria for determining this status include:<br>• Being a legal entity.<br>• Having a distinct market or client type (e.g., institutional, retail, or private client).<br>• Using a separate and distinct investment process. |
| **DISTRIBUTION** | Cash or stock distributed to LIMITED PARTNERS (or investors) from an investment vehicle. DISTRIBUTIONS are typically at the discretion of the GENERAL PARTNER (or the FIRM). DISTRIBUTIONS include both recallable and non-recallable DISTRIBUTIONS. |
| **DPI (REALIZATION MULTIPLE)** | SINCE-INCEPTION DISTRIBUTIONS divided by SINCE-INCEPTION PAID-IN CAPITAL. |
| **EX ANTE** | Before the fact. |
| **EX POST** | After the fact. |
| **EXPENSE RATIO** | The ratio of total POOLED FUND expenses to average net assets. The EXPENSE RATIO SHOULD NOT reflect TRANSACTION COSTS. |
| **EXTERNAL CASH FLOW** | Capital (cash or investments) that enters or exits a PORTFOLIO. Dividend and interest income payments are not considered EXTERNAL CASH FLOWS. |
| **EXTERNAL VALUATION** | An assessment of value performed by an independent third party. |
| **FAIR VALUE** | The amount at which an investment could be sold in an arm's-length transaction between willing parties in an orderly transaction. The valuation MUST be determined using the objective, observable, unadjusted quoted market price for an identical investment in an active market on the measurement date, if available. In the absence of an objective, observable, unadjusted quoted market price for an identical investment in an active market on the measurement date, the valuation MUST represent the FIRM's best estimate of the FAIR VALUE. FAIR VALUE MUST include any accrued income. |
| **FEE SCHEDULE** | The FIRM's current schedule of INVESTMENT MANAGEMENT FEES or BUNDLED FEES appropriate to PROSPECTIVE CLIENTS or PROSPECTIVE INVESTORS. |

*(continued)*



 

| | |
|---|---|
| **FIRM** | The entity defined for compliance with the GIPS standards. |
| **FIXED COMMITMENT** | Having a predetermined amount of COMMITTED CAPITAL. |
| **FIXED LIFE** | Having a predetermined, finite investment time horizon. |
| **GENERAL PARTNER** | Typically, the manager of a LIMITED PARTNERSHIP in which the LIMITED PARTNERS are the other investors. The GENERAL PARTNER earns an INVESTMENT MANAGEMENT FEE that may include a percentage of the LIMITED PARTNERSHIP'S profits. (See "CARRIED INTEREST.") |
| **GIPS ADVERTISEMENT** | An advertisement by a GIPS-compliant FIRM that adheres to the REQUIREMENTS of the GIPS Advertising Guidelines. |
| **GIPS COMPLIANCE NOTIFICATION FORM** | The form REQUIRED to be filed with CFA Institute to notify CFA Institute that the FIRM claims compliance with the GIPS standards. |
| **GIPS COMPOSITE REPORT** | A presentation for a COMPOSITE that contains all the information REQUIRED by the GIPS standards and may also include RECOMMENDED information or SUPPLEMENTAL INFORMATION. |
| **GIPS POOLED FUND REPORT** | A presentation for a POOLED FUND that contains all the information REQUIRED by the GIPS standards and may also include RECOMMENDED information or SUPPLEMENTAL INFORMATION. |
| **GIPS REPORT** | Either a GIPS COMPOSITE REPORT or a GIPS POOLED FUND REPORT. |
| **GROSS-OF-FEES** | The return on investments reduced by any TRANSACTION COSTS. |
| **HIGH WATERMARK** | The return or value that a POOLED FUND or SEGREGATED ACCOUNT MUST exceed for the FIRM to be entitled to earn a PERFORMANCE-BASED FEE. |
| **HURDLE RATE** | Minimum rate of return that a POOLED FUND or SEGREGATED ACCOUNT MUST exceed in order for the investment manager to be able to accrue a PERFORMANCE-BASED FEE. |
| **ILLIQUID INVESTMENTS** | Investments that may be difficult to sell without a price reduction or that cannot be sold quickly because of a lack of market or ready/willing investors. |
| **INCOME RETURN** | The investment income earned on all investments (including cash and cash equivalents) during the measurement period, net of all non-recoverable expenditures, interest expense on debt, and property taxes. The INCOME RETURN is computed as a percentage of the CAPITAL EMPLOYED. |

  

| | |
|---|---|
| **INTERNAL DISPERSION** | A measure of the spread of the annual returns of individual PORTFOLIOS within a COMPOSITE. Measures may include, but are not limited to, high/low, range, and STANDARD DEVIATION (asset weighted or equal weighted) of PORTFOLIO returns. |
| **INVESTMENT MANAGEMENT FEE** | The fee payable to the FIRM for management of a PORTFOLIO. INVESTMENT MANAGEMENT FEES are typically asset based (percentage of assets), performance based (see "PERFORMANCE-BASED FEE"), or a combination of the two but may take different forms as well. INVESTMENT MANAGEMENT FEES also include CARRIED INTEREST. |
| **INVESTMENT MULTIPLE (TVPI)** | TOTAL VALUE divided by SINCE-INCEPTION PAID-IN CAPITAL. |
| **LARGE CASH FLOW** | The level at which the FIRM determines that an EXTERNAL CASH FLOW may distort the return if the PORTFOLIO is not valued and a sub-period return is not calculated. The FIRM MUST define the amount in terms of the value of cash/asset flow or in terms of a percentage of the PORTFOLIO assets or COMPOSITE assets. The FIRM MUST also determine if a LARGE CASH FLOW is a single EXTERNAL CASH FLOW or an aggregate of a number of EXTERNAL CASH FLOWS within a stated period. |
| **LIMITED DISTRIBUTION POOLED FUND** | Any POOLED FUND that is not a BROAD DISTRIBUTION POOLED FUND. |
| **LIMITED PARTNER** | An investor in a LIMITED PARTNERSHIP. |
| **LIMITED PARTNERSHIP** | The legal structure used by many PRIVATE MARKET INVESTMENT CLOSED-END POOLED FUNDS. LIMITED PARTNERSHIPS are usually FIXED LIFE investment vehicles. The GENERAL PARTNER manages the LIMITED PARTNERSHIP pursuant to the partnership agreement. |
| **LINK** | The method by which sub-period returns are geometrically combined to calculate the period return, or by which periodic returns are geometrically combined to calculate longer-period returns, using the following formula: $\text{Period return} = [(1 + R_1) \times (1 + R_2) \ldots (1 + R_n)] - 1$ where $R_1, R_2 \ldots R_n$ are the sub-period or periodic returns for sub-periods or periods 1 through $n$, respectively. |
| **MARKET VALUE** | The price at which investors can buy or sell an investment at a given time multiplied by the quantity held, plus any accrued income. |
| **MATERIAL ERROR** | An error in a GIPS COMPOSITE REPORT or GIPS POOLED FUND REPORT that MUST be corrected and disclosed in a corrected GIPS COMPOSITE REPORT or GIPS POOLED FUND REPORT. |

*(continued)*

**MINIMUM EFFECTIVE COMPLIANCE DATE** — The date after which a FIRM may present only GIPS-compliant performance. REAL ESTATE and PRIVATE EQUITY COMPOSITES and POOLED FUNDS and WRAP FEE COMPOSITES have a MINIMUM EFFECTIVE COMPLIANCE DATE of 1 January 2006. All other COMPOSITES and POOLED FUNDS have a MINIMUM EFFECTIVE COMPLIANCE DATE of 1 January 2000.

**MONEY-WEIGHTED RETURN (MWR)** — The return for a period that reflects the change in value and the timing and size of EXTERNAL CASH FLOWS.

**MUST** — A provision, task, or action that is mandatory or REQUIRED to be followed or performed. (See "REQUIRE/REQUIREMENT.")

**MUST NOT** — A task or action that is forbidden or prohibited.

**NET-OF-FEES** — The GROSS-OF-FEES return reduced by INVESTMENT MANAGEMENT FEES.

**OPEN-END FUND** — A POOLED FUND in which the number of investors is not fixed and the fund is open for subscriptions and/or redemptions.

**OVERLAY EXPOSURE** — The economic value for which a FIRM has investment management responsibility. OVERLAY EXPOSURE is the notional value of the OVERLAY STRATEGY being managed, the value of the underlying PORTFOLIOS being overlaid, or a specified target exposure.

**OVERLAY STRATEGY** — A strategy in which the management of a certain aspect of an investment strategy is carried out separately from the underlying PORTFOLIO. OVERLAY STRATEGIES are typically designed either to limit or maintain a specified risk exposure that is present in the underlying PORTFOLIO or to profit from a tactical view on the market by changing a PORTFOLIO's specified risk exposure.

**PAID-IN CAPITAL** — Capital inflows to a POOLED FUND or COMPOSITE. It includes COMMITTED CAPITAL drawn down through capital calls and DISTRIBUTIONS that are subsequently recalled and reinvested.

**PERFORMANCE-BASED FEE** — A type of INVESTMENT MANAGEMENT FEE that is typically based on the PORTFOLIO's performance on an absolute basis or relative to a BENCHMARK or other reference point.

**PERFORMANCE-BASED FEE DESCRIPTION** — General information regarding the PERFORMANCE-BASED FEE. It MUST include enough information to allow a PROSPECTIVE CLIENT or PROSPECTIVE INVESTOR to understand the key characteristics of the PERFORMANCE-BASED FEE. It MUST include relevant information (e.g., PERFORMANCE-BASED FEE RATE, HURDLE RATE, CLAWBACK, HIGH WATERMARK, reset frequency, accrual frequency, CRYSTALLIZATION SCHEDULE) and on what basis fees are charged.

  

**PERFORMANCE EXAMINATION** — A process by which an independent verifier conducts testing of a specific COMPOSITE or POOLED FUND in accordance with the REQUIRED PERFORMANCE EXAMINATION procedures of the GIPS standards.

**PERFORMANCE EXAMINATION REPORT** — A report issued by an independent verifier after a PERFORMANCE EXAMINATION has been performed.

**PERFORMANCE-RELATED INFORMATION** — Includes:

- Information expressed in terms of investment return and risk.
- Other information and input data that directly relate to the calculation of investment return and risk (e.g., PORTFOLIO holdings), as well as information derived from investment return and risk input data (e.g., performance contribution or attribution).

**PERIODICITY** — The length of the period over which a variable is measured (e.g., a variable measured at a monthly PERIODICITY consists of observations for each month).

**PIC MULTIPLE** — SINCE-INCEPTION PAID-IN CAPITAL divided by cumulative COMMITTED CAPITAL.

**POOLED FUND** — A fund whose ownership interests may be held by more than one investor.

**POOLED FUND DESCRIPTION** — General information regarding the investment mandate, objective, or strategy of the POOLED FUND. The POOLED FUND DESCRIPTION MUST include enough information to allow a PROSPECTIVE INVESTOR to understand the key characteristics of the POOLED FUND's investment mandate, objective, or strategy, including:

- The material risks of the POOLED FUND's strategy.
- How leverage, derivatives, and short positions may be used, if they are a material part of the strategy.
- If ILLIQUID INVESTMENTS are a material part of the strategy.

**POOLED FUND GROSS RETURN** — The return on investments reduced by any TRANSACTION COSTS.

**POOLED FUND INCEPTION DATE** — The date when the POOLED FUND's track record starts.

For a LIMITED DISTRIBUTION POOLED FUND, the POOLED FUND INCEPTION DATE may be based on the following dates:

- When INVESTMENT MANAGEMENT FEES are first charged.
- When the first investment-related cash flow takes place.
- When the first capital call is made.
- When the first COMMITTED CAPITAL is closed and legally binding.

*(continued)*



 

**POOLED FUND NET RETURN** — The POOLED FUND GROSS RETURN reduced by all fees and expenses, including INVESTMENT MANAGEMENT FEES, ADMINISTRATIVE FEES, and other costs.

**POOLED FUND OF FUNDS** — An investment vehicle that invests in underlying investment vehicles.

**POOLED FUND TERMINATION DATE** — The date when the POOLED FUND'S assets have all been distributed, or when investment discretion ends.

**PORTFOLIO** — An individually managed group of investments. A PORTFOLIO may be a SEGREGATED ACCOUNT or a POOLED FUND, including assets managed by a SUB-ADVISOR for which the FIRM has discretion over the selection of the SUB-ADVISOR.

**PORTFOLIO-WEIGHTED CUSTOM BENCHMARK** — A BENCHMARK created using the BENCHMARKS of the individual PORTFOLIOS in the COMPOSITE.

**PRIMARY FUND** — An investment vehicle that makes DIRECT INVESTMENTS rather than investing in other investment vehicles.

**PRIVATE EQUITY** — Investment strategies include, but are not limited to, venture capital, leveraged buyouts, consolidations, mezzanine and distressed debt investments, and a variety of hybrids, such as venture leasing and venture factoring.

**PRIVATE MARKET INVESTMENTS** — Includes real assets (e.g., REAL ESTATE and infrastructure), PRIVATE EQUITY, and similar investments that are illiquid, not publicly traded, and not traded on an exchange.

**PROPRIETARY ASSETS** — Investments owned by the FIRM, the FIRM'S management, and/or the FIRM'S parent company that are managed by the FIRM. GENERAL PARTNER assets in a POOLED FUND are considered PROPRIETARY ASSETS.

**PROSPECTIVE CLIENT** — Any person or entity that has expressed interest in one of the FIRM'S COMPOSITE strategies and qualifies to invest in the COMPOSITE. Current clients may also qualify as PROSPECTIVE CLIENTS for any COMPOSITE strategy that differs from their current investment strategy. Investment consultants and other third parties are included as PROSPECTIVE CLIENTS if they represent individuals or entities that qualify as PROSPECTIVE CLIENTS.

**PROSPECTIVE INVESTOR** — Any person or entity that has expressed interest in one of the FIRM'S POOLED FUNDS and qualifies to invest in the POOLED FUND. Current POOLED FUND investors may also qualify as PROSPECTIVE INVESTORS for any POOLED FUND that differs from their current POOLED FUND. Investment consultants and other third parties are included as PROSPECTIVE INVESTORS if they represent individuals or entities that qualify as PROSPECTIVE INVESTORS.

  

| | |
|---|---|
| **PUBLIC MARKET EQUIVALENT (PME)** | The performance of a public market index expressed in terms of a MONEY-WEIGHTED RETURN (MWR), using the same cash flows and timing as those of the COMPOSITE OR POOLED FUND over the same period. A PME can be used as a BENCHMARK by comparing the MWR of a COMPOSITE OR POOLED FUND with the PME of a public market index. |
| **PURE GROSS-OF-FEES** | The return on investments that is not reduced by any TRANSACTION COSTS incurred during the period. |
| **REAL ESTATE** | REAL ESTATE includes wholly owned or partially owned:<br>• Investments in land, including products grown from the land (e.g., timber or crops).<br>• Buildings under development, completed buildings, and other structures or improvements.<br>• Equity-oriented debt (e.g., participating mortgage loans).<br>• Private interest in a property for which some portion of the return to the investor at the time of investment relates to the performance of the underlying REAL ESTATE. |
| **REALIZATION MULTIPLE (DPI)** | SINCE-INCEPTION DISTRIBUTIONS divided by SINCE-INCEPTION PAID-IN CAPITAL. |
| **RECOMMEND/ RECOMMENDATION** | A suggested provision, task, or action that SHOULD be followed or performed. A RECOMMENDATION is considered to be best practice but is not a REQUIREMENT. (See "SHOULD.") |
| **REQUIRE/REQUIREMENT** | A provision, task, or action that MUST be followed or performed. |
| **RESIDUAL VALUE** | The remaining equity that LIMITED PARTNERS or investors have in an investment vehicle at the end of the performance reporting period. |
| **RVPI (UNREALIZED MULTIPLE)** | RESIDUAL VALUE divided by SINCE-INCEPTION PAID-IN CAPITAL. |
| **SALES CHARGES AND LOADS** | The costs associated with buying or selling shares of a POOLED FUND. These costs may also be known as subscription and redemption costs or as entry and exit fees. |
| **SEGREGATED ACCOUNT** | A PORTFOLIO owned by a single client. |
| **SHOULD** | A provision, task, or action that is RECOMMENDED to be followed or performed and is considered to be best practice but is not REQUIRED. |
| **SHOULD NOT** | A task or action that is RECOMMENDED not to be followed or performed and is considered best practice not to do so. |

*(continued)*

**SIDE POCKET**

A type of account used mainly in alternative investment POOLED FUNDS to separate ILLIQUID INVESTMENTS or distressed assets from other, more liquid investments or to segregate investments held for a special purpose from other investments. SIDE POCKETS are typically not available for investing for new POOLED FUND investors that invest after the SIDE POCKET was created.

**SIGNIFICANT CASH FLOW**

The level at which the FIRM determines that one or more client-directed EXTERNAL CASH FLOWS may temporarily prevent the FIRM from implementing the COMPOSITE strategy. The cash flow may be defined by the FIRM as a single flow or an aggregate of a number of flows within a stated period. The measure of significance MUST be determined as either a specific monetary amount (e.g., €50,000,000) or a percentage of PORTFOLIO assets (based on the most recent valuation), and no other criteria, such as the effect of the cash flow or the number of PORTFOLIOS in the COMPOSITE, may be considered. Transfers of assets between asset classes within a PORTFOLIO or FIRM-initiated cash flows MUST NOT be considered SIGNIFICANT CASH FLOWS.

**SINCE-INCEPTION**

For COMPOSITES, from the COMPOSITE INCEPTION DATE.

For POOLED FUNDS, from the POOLED FUND INCEPTION DATE.

**STANDARD DEVIATION**

A measure of the variability of returns. As a measure of INTERNAL DISPERSION, STANDARD DEVIATION quantifies the distribution of the individual PORTFOLIOS' returns within the COMPOSITE. As a measure of historical risk, STANDARD DEVIATION quantifies the variability of the COMPOSITE, POOLED FUND, or BENCHMARK returns over time. Also referred to as "external STANDARD DEVIATION."

**SUB-ADVISOR**

A third-party investment manager hired by the FIRM to manage some or all of the assets for which a FIRM has investment management responsibility. May also be referred to as a sub-manager or third-party investment manager.

**SUBSCRIPTION LINE OF CREDIT**

A loan facility that is put in place to facilitate administration when the FIRM is calling for funds from investors. Alternatively, it can be used in lieu of calling funds from investors.

**SUPPLEMENTAL INFORMATION**

Any PERFORMANCE-RELATED INFORMATION included as part of a GIPS COMPOSITE REPORT or GIPS POOLED FUND REPORT that supplements or enhances the REQUIREMENTS and/or RECOMMENDATIONS of the GIPS standards.

  

| | |
|---|---|
| **TEMPORARY NEW ACCOUNT** | An account for temporarily holding client-directed EXTERNAL CASH FLOWS until they are invested according to the COMPOSITE strategy or disbursed. A FIRM can use a TEMPORARY NEW ACCOUNT to remove the effect of a SIGNIFICANT CASH FLOW on a PORTFOLIO. When a SIGNIFICANT CASH FLOW occurs in a PORTFOLIO, the FIRM may direct the EXTERNAL CASH FLOW to a TEMPORARY NEW ACCOUNT according to the COMPOSITE'S SIGNIFICANT CASH FLOW policy. |
| **THEORETICAL PERFORMANCE** | Performance that is not derived from a PORTFOLIO or COMPOSITE with actual assets invested in the strategy presented. THEORETICAL PERFORMANCE includes model, backtested, hypothetical, simulated, indicative, EX ANTE, and forward-looking performance. |
| **TIME-WEIGHTED RETURN (TWR)** | A method of calculating period-by-period returns that reflects the change in value and negates the effects of EXTERNAL CASH FLOWS. |
| **TOTAL FIRM ASSETS** | All discretionary and non-discretionary assets for which a FIRM has investment management responsibility. TOTAL FIRM ASSETS include assets assigned to a SUB-ADVISOR provided the FIRM has discretion over the selection of the SUB-ADVISOR. |
| **TOTAL POOLED FUND FEES** | All fees and expenses charged to the POOLED FUND, including but not limited to INVESTMENT MANAGEMENT FEES and ADMINISTRATIVE FEES. |
| **TOTAL RETURN** | The rate of return that includes the realized and unrealized gains and losses plus income for the measurement period. |
| **TOTAL VALUE** | RESIDUAL VALUE plus DISTRIBUTIONS. |
| **TRADE DATE ACCOUNTING** | Recognizing the asset or liability on the date of the purchase or sale and not on the settlement date. Recognizing the asset or liability within three business days of the date upon which the transaction is entered (trade date, T + 1, T + 2, or T + 3) satisfies the TRADE DATE ACCOUNTING REQUIREMENT for purposes of the GIPS standards. |
| **TRANSACTION COSTS** | The costs of buying or selling investments. These costs typically take the form of brokerage commissions, exchange fees and/or taxes, and/or bid–offer spreads from either internal or external brokers. Custodial fees charged per transaction SHOULD be considered CUSTODY FEES and not TRANSACTION COSTS. For REAL ESTATE, PRIVATE EQUITY, and other PRIVATE MARKET INVESTMENTS, TRANSACTION COSTS include all legal, financial, advisory, and investment banking fees related to buying, selling, restructuring, and/or recapitalizing investments but do not include dead deal costs. |

*(continued)*

| | |
|---|---|
| **TVPI (INVESTMENT MULTIPLE)** | TOTAL VALUE divided by SINCE-INCEPTION PAID-IN CAPITAL. |
| **UNREALIZED MULTIPLE (RVPI)** | RESIDUAL VALUE divided by SINCE-INCEPTION PAID-IN CAPITAL. |
| **VERIFICATION** | A process by which an independent verifier conducts testing of a FIRM on a FIRM-wide basis, in accordance with the REQUIRED VERIFICATION procedures of the GIPS standards. |
| **VERIFICATION REPORT** | A report issued by an independent verifier after a VERIFICATION has been performed. |
| **VINTAGE YEAR** | Two methods used to determine VINTAGE YEAR are:<br>1. The year of the investment vehicle's first drawdown or capital call from its investors.<br>2. The year when the first COMMITTED CAPITAL from outside investors is closed and legally binding. |
| **WRAP FEE** | A type of BUNDLED FEE specific to a particular investment product. The WRAP FEE is charged by a WRAP FEE sponsor for investment management services and typically includes associated TRANSACTION COSTS that cannot be separately identified. WRAP FEES can be all-inclusive, asset-based fees and may include a combination of INVESTMENT MANAGEMENT FEES, TRANSACTION COSTS, CUSTODY FEES, and/or ADMINISTRATIVE FEES. A WRAP FEE PORTFOLIO is sometimes referred to as a "separately managed account" (SMA) or "managed account." |

  

# APPENDIX A: SAMPLE GIPS COMPOSITE REPORTS

**SAMPLE 1 COMPOSITE WITH TIME-WEIGHTED RETURNS**

**Spinning Top Investments**
**Large Cap Growth Composite**
**1 February 2011 to 31 December 2020**

| Year | Composite Gross Return TWR (%) | Composite Net Return TWR (%) | Benchmark Return (%) | 3-Year Std Deviation: Composite Gross (%) | 3-Year Std Deviation: Benchmark (%) | Number of Portfolios | Internal Dispersion (%) | Composite Assets ($ M) | Firm Assets[b] ($ M) |
|---|---|---|---|---|---|---|---|---|---|
| 2011[a] | 2.18 | 1.25 | 1.17 | | | 31 | n/a | 165 | n/a |
| 2012 | 18.66 | 17.49 | 15.48 | | | 34 | 2.0 | 235 | n/a |
| 2013 | 41.16 | 39.80 | 33.36 | | | 38 | 5.7 | 344 | n/a |
| 2014 | 14.50 | 13.37 | 13.03 | 11.30 | 9.59 | 45 | 2.8 | 445 | 1,032 |
| 2015 | 6.52 | 5.47 | 5.67 | 12.51 | 10.68 | 48 | 3.1 | 520 | 1,056 |
| 2016 | 8.22 | 7.15 | 7.09 | 12.95 | 11.15 | 49 | 2.8 | 505 | 1,185 |
| 2017 | 33.78 | 32.48 | 30.18 | 12.29 | 10.53 | 44 | 2.9 | 475 | 1,269 |
| 2018 | −0.84 | −1.83 | −0.65 | 13.26 | 11.91 | 47 | 3.1 | 493 | 1,091 |
| 2019 | 33.08 | 31.78 | 29.76 | 12.81 | 11.71 | 51 | 3.5 | 549 | 1,252 |
| 2020 | 7.51 | 6.44 | 6.30 | 13.74 | 12.37 | 54 | 2.5 | 575 | 1,414 |

[a] Returns are for the period 1 February 2011 to 31 December 2011.

[b] Spinning Top Investments acquired the composite through an acquisition of ABC Capital in May 2014. Firm assets prior to 2014 are not presented because the composite was not part of the firm.

## Disclosures

1. Spinning Top Investments claims compliance with the Global Investment Performance Standards (GIPS®) and has prepared and presented this report in compliance with the GIPS standards. Spinning Top Investments has been independently verified for the periods 1 January 2011 to 31 December 2020. The verification report is available upon request.

   A firm that claims compliance with the GIPS standards must establish policies and procedures for complying with all the applicable requirements of the GIPS standards. Verification provides assurance on whether the firm's policies and procedures related to composite and pooled fund maintenance, as well as the calculation, presentation, and distribution of performance, have been designed in compliance with the GIPS standards and have been implemented on a firm-wide basis. Verification does not provide assurance on the accuracy of any specific performance report.

2. Spinning Top Investments is an equity investment manager that invests solely in US-based securities. Spinning Top Investments is defined as an independent investment management firm that is not affiliated with any parent organization. Spinning Top Investments acquired ABC Capital in May 2014.
3. The Large Cap Growth Composite includes all institutional portfolios that invest in large-cap US stocks that are considered to have growth in earnings prospects that are superior to that of the average company within the XYZ Large Cap Growth Index. Key material risks include the risks that stock prices will decline and that the composite will underperform its benchmark. The account minimum for the composite is $5 million. Prior to July 2016, the account minimum was $2 million. Prior to March 2020, the name of the composite was the Growth Composite.
4. Performance prior to May 2014 occurred while the investment management team was affiliated with another firm. The investment management team has managed the composite since its inception, and the investment process has not changed. The historical performance has been linked to performance earned at Spinning Top Investments.
5. The benchmark is the XYZ Large Cap Growth Index, a market-capitalization-weighted equity index of all US stocks with a market cap greater than $10 billion and a growth tilt.
6. Returns presented are time-weighted returns. Valuations are computed and performance is reported in US dollars.
7. Gross-of-fees returns are presented before management and custodial fees but after all trading expenses. Composite and benchmark returns are presented gross of non-reclaimable withholding taxes. Net-of-fees returns are calculated by deducting a model management fee of 0.083%, 1/12th of the highest management fee of 1.00%, from the monthly gross composite return. The management fee schedule for separate accounts is as follows: 1.00% on the first $25 million; 0.60% thereafter. The management fee schedule and total expense ratio for the Large Cap Collective Fund, which is included in the composite, are 0.65% on all assets and 0.93%, respectively.
8. Policies for valuing investments, calculating performance, and preparing GIPS reports are available upon request.
9. A list of composite descriptions and a list of broad distribution pooled funds are available upon request.
10. The composite was created in November 2011, and the inception date is 1 February 2011.
11. As of 1 January 2014, internal dispersion is calculated using the equal-weighted standard deviation of annual gross returns of those portfolios that were included in the composite for the entire year. Prior to 2014, internal dispersion was calculated using asset-weighted standard deviation.

  

12. The three-year annualized standard deviation measures the variability of the composite gross returns and the benchmark returns over the preceding 36-month period.
13. Effective November 1, 2011, portfolios are removed from the composite if they have a significant cash flow. A significant cash flow is defined as a contribution or withdrawal greater than 25% of the beginning market value of a portfolio. The portfolio is removed from the composite for the month in which the significant cash flow occurred.
14. GIPS® is a registered trademark of CFA Institute. CFA Institute does not endorse or promote this organization, nor does it warrant the accuracy or quality of the content contained herein.

## SAMPLE 2 COMPOSITE WITH MONEY-WEIGHTED RETURNS

**Able Management Company**
**Global Absolute Return Composite**
**Reporting Currency: EUR**

| | Annualized Since-Inception MWR (%) | | | | | |
|---|---|---|---|---|---|---|
| Period End | Composite Gross | Composite Net | Custom Benchmark | Number of Portfolios | Composite Assets (€ M) | Total Firm Assets (€ M) |
| 31 Dec 2020* | 7.4 | 6.9 | 5.9 | 8 | 252 | 11,203 |

*Money-weighted returns are for the period from 1 July 2012 (composite inception date) to 31 December 2020.

Able Management Company claims compliance with the Global Investment Performance Standards (GIPS®) and has prepared and presented this report in compliance with the GIPS standards. Able Management Company has not been independently verified.

## Disclosures

1. **Definition of the Firm**

   Able Management Company is an independent investment management firm established in 2007. Able Management Company manages a variety of equity, fixed-income, and balanced assets, primarily for European clients.

2. **Composite Description**

   Able Management Company's Global Absolute Return Composite is a fixed life strategy that uses a global macro approach to find what we believe are deep value–based equity and fixed-income securities. We look for value among beaten-down equity and fixed-income securities, including both investment-grade and non-investment-grade bonds, and may use currency forwards to add value or for hedging purposes. Key risks: The burden of national debt, high political risks, and a possible change in monetary policy by central banks may derail the economy. Because investments include both investment- and non-investment-grade debt, there is also the risk that credit events may affect the valuation and repayment of principal and interest. Fixed-income securities are also subject to interest rate risk, sector and/or country risk, and industry risk. Equity securities are subject to several risks including market risk, company-specific event risk, or becoming worthless in the case of bankruptcy. The strategy invests in currency forwards not only for hedging purposes but also for alpha generation. There is risk that currency bets may not work in our favor as a result of political events, central bank intervention, or other factors not foreseen. The investments are expected to be liquidated in December 2022, and all proceeds will be distributed at that time. The composite was created in January 2013.

3. **Custom Benchmark**

   The benchmark is calculated using a modified public market equivalent (PME) of the XYZ Global Macro Index, where capital calls are treated as cash flows to buy the index. Rather than treat distributions as cash flows to sell the index, we compute the weight of the distribution and remove the same weight. This modification tackles the negative net asset value (NAV) limitation that can occur with the traditional Long–Nickels PME calculation. The XYZ Global Macro Index consists of the median returns of global macro hedge funds that typically invest in long and short positions in international stocks and bonds, commodities, and currencies.

4. **Fees**

   Gross returns are gross of management fees, custodial fees, and withholding taxes but net of all transaction costs. Net returns are net of actual management fees and transaction costs but gross of custodial fees and withholding taxes.

5. **Sub-Advisor**

   A sub-advisor was used since the composite's inception to manage all equity investments.

6. **Fee Schedule**

   The standard fixed annual management fee is 0.55% up to €50 million and 0.35% thereafter.

7. **External Cash Flows**

   Effective 1 January 2020, money-weighted return (MWR) calculations use daily cash flows. Prior to this date, external cash flows were recorded quarterly.

8. **Policies**

   Able Management Company's policies for valuing investments, calculating performance, and preparing GIPS reports are available upon request.

  

**9. List of Composites and Pooled Funds**

A list including composite descriptions, pooled fund descriptions for limited distribution pooled funds, and broad distribution funds is available upon request.

**10. Change in Composite Returns**

Given the fixed life nature of the strategy and the fact that we control the timing of cash flows to and from portfolios, we changed the type of composite returns that are presented. Effective 1 January 2020, we changed from presenting time-weighted returns (TWRs) to MWR because the firm believes it is the most appropriate composite return.

**11. Error Correction**

An incorrect amount was previously used for a cash distribution that occurred in 2020. The since-inception annualized gross and net composite returns have been restated from 8.4% and 7.9% to 7.4% and 6.9%, respectively.

**12. Trademark**

GIPS® is a registered trademark of CFA Institute. CFA Institute does not endorse or promote this organization, nor does it warrant the accuracy or quality of the content contained herein.

## SAMPLE 3 WRAP FEE COMPOSITE WITH TIME-WEIGHTED RETURNS

**ABC Investments**
**Small Cap Value Wrap Composite**
**January 1, 2011 to December 31, 2020**

| Year | Pure Gross Return[a] (%) | Gross Return (%) | Net Return (%) | Benchmark Return (%) | Internal Dispersion (%) | Number of Portfolios | Composite Assets ($ M) | Firm Assets ($ M) |
|---|---|---|---|---|---|---|---|---|
| 2020 | 28.84 | 28.72 | 25.10 | 23.75 | 0.7 | 2,368 | 1,015 | 18,222 |
| 2019 | 12.30 | 12.20 | 9.01 | 9.79 | 1.1 | 1,730 | 687 | 17,635 |
| 2018 | 17.57 | 17.47 | 14.14 | 14.56 | 1.0 | 1,462 | 432 | 19,246 |
| 2017 | 10.55 | 10.45 | 7.30 | 7.84 | 1.2 | 928 | 321 | 14,819 |
| 2016 | 39.05 | 38.93 | 35.04 | 31.74 | 0.9 | 649 | 163 | 12,362 |
| 2015 | -6.75 | -6.75 | -9.53 | -7.47 | 0.8 | 68 | 1,115 | 7,051 |
| 2014 | 6.64 | 6.64 | 3.50 | 4.22 | 1.0 | 52 | 1,110 | 6,419 |
| 2013 | 45.86 | 45.86 | 41.68 | 34.50 | 1.1 | 46 | 990 | 5,612 |
| 2012 | 24.41 | 24.41 | 20.79 | 18.05 | 0.9 | 38 | 975 | 4,422 |
| 2011 | -4.90 | -4.90 | -7.73 | -5.50 | 0.8 | 41 | 870 | 3,632 |

| Year | Composite Pure Gross 3-Yr Annualized Ex Post Std Dev (%) | Benchmark 3-Yr Annualized Ex Post Std Dev (%) | Percentage of Wrap-Fee Portfolios (%) | Strategy Advisory-Only Assets[(b)] ($ M) | Firm Advisory-Only Assets[(b)] ($ M) |
|---|---|---|---|---|---|
| 2020 | 13.44 | 12.58 | 100 | 349 | 1,822 |
| 2019 | 11.52 | 10.98 | 100 | 232 | 1,764 |
| 2018 | 13.99 | 12.62 | 100 | 102 | 1,925 |
| 2017 | 15.75 | 13.97 | 100 | 68 | 1,482 |
| 2016 | 17.49 | 15.50 | 100 | 32 | 1,236 |
| 2015 | 15.52 | 13.46 | 0 | 0 | 0 |
| 2014 | 14.91 | 12.79 | 0 | 0 | 0 |
| 2013 | 18.82 | 15.82 | 0 | 0 | 0 |
| 2012 | 22.65 | 19.89 | 0 | 0 | 0 |
| 2011 | 29.31 | 26.05 | 0 | 0 | 0 |

[(a)] Effective January 1, 2016, pure gross returns do not reflect the deduction of any expenses, including transaction costs, and are supplemental information. See Note 6.

[(b)] Strategy and firm advisory-only assets are supplemental information. See Note 9.

1. ABC Investments is an independent investment adviser registered under the Investment Advisers Act of 1940 and was founded in March 1996. The firm was redefined in January 2016 to include institutional and wrap accounts. Prior to January 2016, the firm included only institutional accounts.
2. ABC Investments claims compliance with the Global Investment Performance Standards (GIPS®) and has prepared and presented this report in compliance with the GIPS standards. ABC Investments has been independently verified for the period from April 1, 1996 through December 31, 2020. A firm that claims compliance with the GIPS standards must establish policies and procedures for complying with all the applicable requirements of the GIPS standards. Verification provides assurance on whether the firm's policies and procedures related to composite and pooled fund maintenance, as well as the calculation, presentation, and distribution of performance, have been designed in compliance with the GIPS standards and have been implemented on a firm-wide basis. The Small Cap Value Wrap Composite has had a performance examination for the period from 1 January 2016 through 31 December 2020. The verification and performance examination reports are available upon request.
3. The Small Cap Value Wrap Composite is composed of portfolios invested in US equities that have a market capitalization of between $500 million and $2 billion at purchase. Historically, small-cap stocks have been more volatile than large-cap stocks. Effective January 1, 2016, the composite was redefined to include only wrap fee accounts. Prior to the redefinition, the composite included only institutional accounts. Performance results

  

prior to 2016 are those of the Small Cap Value Institutional Composite. Wrap accounts are charged a wrap fee that is based not on transactions in a client's account but is based on a percentage of account assets. The composite inception date is February 1, 2006. The composite was created in March 2016.

4. All returns are calculated and presented in US dollars. Policies for valuing investments, calculating performance, and preparing GIPS reports are available upon request. A list of composite descriptions is available upon request.
5. The benchmark is the XYZ Small Cap Value Index and is provided to represent the investment environment existing during the periods shown. The XYZ Small Cap Value Index is a float-adjusted, market-cap-weighted index that measures the performance of the smallest 800 companies traded on US exchanges with low price-to-book ratios that are included in the XYZ 3000 Value Index. The XYZ 3000 Value Index is a float-adjusted, market-cap-weighted index that includes 3,000 of the largest companies traded on US exchanges with low price-to-book ratios. The index is fully invested and includes the reinvestment of income. The returns for the index do not include any trading costs, management fees, or other costs. Index returns have been taken from published sources.
6. Pure gross returns, presented as supplemental information from 2016 through 2020, do not reflect the deduction of any trading costs, fees, or expenses. Pure gross returns prior to 2016 reflect the deduction of transaction costs because performance is from the Small Cap Value Institutional Composite. Effective January 1, 2016, the gross return is calculated by applying a model transaction cost of $0.05 per share to each trade. The firm determined the estimated transaction cost for this composite by calculating the actual average transaction costs for accounts in the firm's Small Cap Value Institutional Composite. Prior to January 2016, gross returns are net of actual trading costs.
7. Net returns are calculated by subtracting the highest applicable wrap fee (3.00% on an annual basis, or 0.25% monthly) on a monthly basis from the pure gross composite monthly return. The standard wrap fee schedule in effect is 3.00% of total assets. Wrap fees include all charges, transaction costs, portfolio management fees, custody fees, and other administrative fees.
8. The internal dispersion is measured by the equal-weighted standard deviation of annual pure gross returns of those portfolios included in the composite for the full year. The three-year annualized standard deviation measures the variability of the composite and the benchmark returns over the preceding 36-month period.
9. Strategy advisory-only assets are assets for which ABC Investments provides investment recommendations to another firm for portfolios managed to the composite strategy but has no control over the implementation of investment decisions or trading authority for the assets. Firm advisory-only assets are assets for all strategies within the firm for which ABC Investments provides investment recommendations but has no control over the implementation of investment decisions or trading authority for the assets. Strategy and firm advisory-only assets are presented as supplemental information.

10. Past performance is not an indicator of future results.
11. GIPS® is a registered trademark of CFA Institute. CFA Institute does not endorse or promote this organization, nor does it warrant the accuracy or quality of the content contained herein.

## SAMPLE 4 OVERLAY COMPOSITE WITH TIME-WEIGHTED RETURNS

**Tumble Management Limited**
**Passive Currency Overlay Composite**

**Composite Characteristics**

**Reporting Currency:** CHF

**Benchmark:** Custom – 100% Hedged

**Description:** The composite includes all institutional and retail passive currency overlay portfolios that aim to hedge the underlying portfolio to the Swiss franc with a tracking error target of 25 bps per annum. Currency forwards traded over the counter have counterparty default risk.

**Composite Inception Date:** 1 July 2011

**Composite Creation Date:** December 2011

| Calendar Year | Composite Gross Return (%) | Custom Benchmark Return (%) | Composite Standard Deviation 3-Yr Annualized (%) | Benchmark Standard Deviation 3-Yr Annualized (%) | Number of Portfolios | Internal Composite Dispersion (%) | Year-End Composite Overlay Exposure (CHF millions) | Year-End Firm Overlay Exposure (CHF millions) |
|---|---|---|---|---|---|---|---|---|
| 2011* | 3.88 | 4.03 | n/a | n/a | 2 | n/a | 357 | 3,068 |
| 2012 | 10.94 | 11.05 | n/a | n/a | 3 | n/a | 370 | 2,385 |
| 2013 | 7.02 | 6.97 | n/a | n/a | 3 | n/a | 357 | 2,070 |
| 2014 | 3.35 | 3.37 | 1.87 | 1.91 | 5 | n/a | 429 | 1,789 |
| 2015 | (13.14) | (13.13) | 3.56 | 3.59 | 6 | n/a | 611 | 2,451 |
| 2016 | 7.98 | 8.16 | 4.01 | 3.99 | 6 | 0.09 | 602 | 3,385 |
| 2017 | 6.70 | 6.75 | 4.26 | 4.25 | 7 | 0.15 | 867 | 5,206 |
| 2018 | (13.89) | (14.06) | 4.17 | 4.17 | 2 | n/a | 203 | 4,820 |
| 2019 | (9.06) | (9.05) | 3.86 | 3.90 | 2 | n/a | 231 | 3,863 |
| 2020 | (7.45) | (7.53) | 3.08 | 3.12 | 2 | n/a | 275 | 3,379 |

*Partial period return for the period 1 July 2011 through 31 December 2011.

  

| As of 31 December 2020 | Composite Gross Return (%) | Benchmark Return (%) |
|---|---|---|
| **1-Year** | (7.45) | (7.53) |
| **3-Year annualized** | (10.18) | (10.26) |
| **5-Year annualized** | (3.45) | (3.55) |
| **Since-inception annualized** | (0.82) | (0.81) |
| **Since-inception cumulative** | (7.55) | (7.39) |

1. **Compliance Statement**

   Tumble Management Limited claims compliance with the Global Investment Performance Standards (GIPS®) and has prepared and presented this report in compliance with the GIPS standards. Tumble Management Limited has been independently verified for the periods 1 January 2014 to 31 December 2020. The verification report is available upon request. A firm that claims compliance with the GIPS standards must establish policies and procedures for complying with all the applicable requirements of the GIPS standards. Verification provides assurance on whether the firm's policies and procedures related to composite and pooled fund maintenance, as well as the calculation, presentation, and distribution of performance, have been designed in compliance with the GIPS standards and have been implemented on a firm-wide basis. Verification does not provide assurance on the accuracy of any specific performance report.

2. **Definition of the Firm**

   Tumble Management Limited is an independent investment management firm that manages currency overlay portfolios for institutional clients and is a regulated company.

3. **Methodology Used to Calculate Overlay Exposure**

   Tumble Management Limited does not manage any of the underlying assets for its overlay portfolio clients. Firm overlay exposure represents the total value of all underlying assets for which Tumble Management Limited has a mandate to manage the currency overlay. Composite overlay exposure represents the total value of all underlying portfolios being overlaid in this composite.

4. **Performance Calculation for Portfolios**

   Portfolio performance is calculated on a contribution from hedges basis, whereby the change in the portfolio's cumulative marked-to-market value is divided by the underlying portfolio value being overlaid at the beginning of the period.

5. **Treatment of Collateral**

   Management of the collateral is not part of the overlay strategy. Therefore, the value of the collateral and any collateral income are not included in the overlay performance calculation.


 

6. **Leverage**

This strategy uses forward currency contracts extensively to sell one currency to invest in another currency, in order to adjust the underlying portfolio's currency exposure. In volatile periods, liquidity and correlations between currencies may influence returns significantly.

7. **Custom Benchmark**

The benchmark is 100% hedged. The benchmark is based on a zero-cost one-month rolling hedge, whereby mid spot rates and one-month bid–offer forward points are applied. The composite custom benchmark is calculated using the benchmarks of the portfolios in the composite and is rebalanced monthly based on the beginning values of the portfolios. As of 31 December 2020, the custom benchmark was composed of 68% XYZ World Index and 32% XYZ World ex-Switzerland Index. The components of the custom benchmark and their underlying weightings for all monthly time periods are available upon request.

8. **Fees**

Performance results are presented gross of investment management fees and net of transaction costs. The performance will be reduced by the fees associated with portfolio management. The standard investment management fee schedule is 0.10% of notional value up to CHF 300 million and 0.05% thereafter.

9. **Ex Post Standard Deviation**

The three-year annualized standard deviation measures the variability of the composite gross returns and the benchmark returns over the preceding 36-month period. The three-year annualized ex post standard deviation for the composite and benchmark is not presented for 2011 through 2013 because the composite had fewer than 36 monthly returns.

10. **Internal Composite Dispersion**

The composite dispersion is measured by the equal-weighted standard deviation of the returns for each portfolio in the composite. The measure of dispersion considers only portfolios included in the composite for the full year. When the composite consists of five or fewer portfolios for the full year, no dispersion measure is presented.

11. **Availability of Information**

A list of composite descriptions is available upon request. Policies for valuing portfolios, calculating performance, and preparing GIPS reports are also available upon request.

12. **Trademark**

GIPS® is a registered trademark of CFA Institute. CFA Institute does not endorse or promote this organization, nor does it warrant the accuracy or quality of the content contained herein.

  

## SAMPLE 5 COMPOSITE WITH CARVE-OUTS WITH ALLOCATED CASH AND TIME-WEIGHTED RETURNS

**Crater Capital**
**High Yield Bond Carve-Out Composite**
**1 January 2011 to 31 December 2020**

| Year | Carve-Out Composite Gross of Fees Return (%) | Carve-Out Composite Net of Fees Return (%) | Benchmark Return (%) | Internal Dispersion | Number of Accounts | Composite Assets ($ M) | Carve-Outs As a % of Composite Assets[a] | Firm Assets ($ M) |
|---|---|---|---|---|---|---|---|---|
| 2020 | 18.33 | 17.82 | 16.57 | 0.46 | 14 | 839 | 82 | 54,382 |
| 2019 | 7.54 | 7.07 | 7.24 | 0.53 | 11 | 680 | 86 | 53,954 |
| 2018 | 4.23 | 3.77 | 4.04 | 0.42 | 12 | 605 | 91 | 50,310 |
| 2017 | 7.73 | 7.26 | 7.21 | n/a | 7 | 553 | 95 | 48,357 |
| 2016 | 18.79 | 18.28 | 16.50 | n/a | ≤5 | 491 | 100 | 45,107 |
| 2015 | -4.59 | -5.01 | -3.98 | n/a | ≤5 | 485 | 100 | 38,719 |
| 2014 | 2.54 | 2.09 | 2.29 | n/a | ≤5 | 384 | 100 | 40,323 |
| 2013 | 7.80 | 7.33 | 6.43 | n/a | ≤5 | 389 | 100 | 39,420 |
| 2012 | 18.32 | 17.81 | 15.08 | n/a | ≤5 | 309 | 100 | 37,039 |
| 2011 | 6.34 | 5.88 | 5.40 | n/a | ≤5 | 213 | 100 | 32,185 |

[a] Represents the percentage of the composite that is composed of carve-outs with allocated cash.

The creation and inception dates of the High Yield Bond Carve-Out Composite are January 2020 and March 2009, respectively.

| | Carve-Out Composite Gross Return 3-Yr Annualized Ex Post St Dev | Benchmark Return 3-Yr Annualized Ex Post St Dev |
|---|---|---|
| 2020 | 6.43 | 6.02 |
| 2019 | 5.11 | 4.88 |
| 2018 | 5.93 | 5.46 |
| 2017 | 6.20 | 5.45 |
| 2016 | 6.66 | 5.87 |
| 2015 | 5.99 | 5.17 |
| 2014 | 5.09 | 4.32 |
| 2013 | 6.72 | 5.64 |
| 2012 | 7.02 | 6.09 |

| High Yield Bond Composite<br>(Composite of Standalone Portfolios)<br>1 January 2017 to 31 December 2020 | | | |
|---|---|---|---|
| | **Standalone Composite Gross of Fees Return (%)** | **Standalone Composite Net of Fees Return (%)** | **Standalone Composite Assets ($ M)** |
| 2020 | 18.25 | 17.71 | 155 |
| 2019 | 6.92 | 6.42 | 93 |
| 2018 | 4.44 | 3.96 | 57 |
| 2017 | 7.11 | 6.62 | 27 |

The inception date of the High Yield Bond Composite is 1 January 2017.

1. Crater Capital claims compliance with the Global Investment Performance Standards (GIPS®) and has prepared and presented this report in compliance with the GIPS standards. Crater Capital has been independently verified for the periods 1 January 2008 to 31 December 2019. The verification report is available upon request.

   A firm that claims compliance with the GIPS standards must establish policies and procedures for complying with all the applicable requirements of the GIPS standards. Verification provides assurance on whether the firm's policies and procedures related to composite and pooled fund maintenance, as well as the calculation, presentation, and distribution of performance, have been designed in compliance with the GIPS standards and have been implemented on a firm-wide basis. Verification does not provide assurance on the accuracy of any specific performance report.

2. For the purpose of complying with the GIPS standards, the firm is defined as Crater Capital, an independent investment advisor registered under the Investment Advisers Act of 1940.

3. The High Yield Bond Carve-Out Composite includes all segregated accounts and high yield bond carve-outs invested in this strategy. The investment objective of the High Yield Bond strategy is to provide investors with a high level of current income. Accounts managed to the strategy will be primarily invested in US high-yield/high-risk fixed-income securities rated BB or lower by a nationally recognized statistical rating organization (NRSRO). Up to 5% of account assets may be invested in investment-grade bonds. High-yield bonds carry increased levels of credit and default risk and are less liquid than government and investment-grade corporate bonds. Some accounts in the composite are carve-outs that have allocated cash. Cash and cash returns are allocated to each account monthly, based on the high-yield segment's beginning value relative to the total portfolio's beginning value, excluding cash. The GIPS Composite Report for the High Yield Bond Composite, which includes only standalone segregated accounts managed to the strategy, is available upon request.

 

4. The composite benchmark is the XYZ US High Yield Corporate Bond Index. The XYZ US High Yield Corporate Bond Index is designed to track the performance of US dollar–denominated, high-yield corporate bonds issued by companies whose country of risk use official G-10 currencies and excludes those countries that are members of the United Nations Eastern European Group. Qualifying securities must have a below-investment-grade rating and maturities of one or more months at purchase. The index is fully invested, which includes the reinvestment of dividends/interest and capital gains. The returns for the index do not include any transaction costs, management fees, or other costs.
5. Composite returns are presented both gross and net of management fees. All composite returns are net of transaction costs and gross of withholding taxes, if any, and reflect the reinvestment of income and other earnings. The composite net-of-fees returns are calculated by deducting 1/12th of the top tier of the management fee schedule (0.50%) from the monthly gross composite return. Actual fees may vary depending on the applicable fee schedule and the size of the account. All returns are calculated and presented in US dollars.
6. The current standard management fee schedule for a segregated account managed to the composite strategy is as follows:
    - 0.50% on the first $50 million.
    - 0.40% on the next $200 million.
    - 0.30% on all assets above $250 million.
7. The internal dispersion is calculated using the asset-weighted standard deviation of account gross returns included in the composite for the full year. For those periods with five or fewer accounts included for the entire year, "n/a" is noted because the dispersion is not considered meaningful.
8. The three-year annualized ex post standard deviation measures the variability of the composite and the benchmark returns over the preceding 36-month period.
9. Policies for valuing investments, calculating performance, and preparing GIPS reports are available upon request. Also available are the List of Composite Descriptions, the List of Pooled Fund Descriptions for Limited Distribution Pooled Funds, and the List of Broad Distribution Pooled Funds.
10. GIPS® is a registered trademark of CFA Institute. CFA Institute does not endorse or promote this organization, nor does it warrant the accuracy or quality of the content contained herein.

# APPENDIX B: SAMPLE GIPS POOLED FUND REPORTS

## SAMPLE 1 POOLED FUND WITH TIME-WEIGHTED RETURNS

**Pudoru Investments**
**Japan Large Cap Equity Fund**
**1 April 2011 to 31 March 2021**

| | | | | 3-Year Annualized Return | | 3-Year Annualized Standard Deviation | | | |
|---|---|---|---|---|---|---|---|---|---|
| 31 March | Fund Gross Return (%) | Fund Net Return (%) | Benchmark Return (%) | Fund Gross (%) | Benchmark (%) | Fund Gross (%) | Benchmark (%) | Fund Assets (¥ B) | Firm Assets (¥ B) |
| 2012 | 2.25 | 1.49 | 2.11 | n/a | n/a | n/a | n/a | 18.4 | 35.1 |
| 2013 | 19.33 | 18.45 | 16.00 | n/a | n/a | n/a | n/a | 29.8 | 51.5 |
| 2014 | 40.20 | 39.18 | 32.39 | 19.60 | 16.18 | 14.22 | 11.94 | 49.7 | 78.6 |
| 2015 | 15.25 | 14.40 | 13.69 | 24.46 | 20.41 | 10.62 | 8.97 | 55.3 | 103.3 |
| 2016 | 1.45 | 0.69 | 1.38 | 17.91 | 15.13 | 12.16 | 10.47 | 57.6 | 124.7 |
| 2017 | 13.53 | 12.69 | 11.96 | 9.90 | 8.87 | 12.04 | 10.60 | 61.8 | 150.8 |
| 2018 | 23.51 | 22.60 | 21.83 | 12.46 | 11.41 | 11.28 | 9.93 | 63.3 | 143.3 |
| 2019 | -8.02 | -8.72 | -7.58 | 8.85 | 8.02 | 12.65 | 11.80 | 49.9 | 146.2 |
| 2020 | -3.86 | -4.58 | -3.67 | 2.98 | 2.74 | 14.20 | 13.56 | 61.6 | 165.6 |
| 2021 | 16.46 | 15.60 | 15.06 | 0.99 | 0.80 | 18.16 | 17.00 | 68.9 | 185.8 |

Pudoru Investments claims compliance with the Global Investment Performance Standards (GIPS®) and has prepared and presented this report in compliance with the GIPS standards. Pudoru Investments has been independently verified for the periods from 1 April 2011 to 31 March 2021. A firm that claims compliance with the GIPS standards must establish policies and procedures for complying with all the applicable requirements of the GIPS standards. Verification provides assurance on whether the firm's policies and procedures related to composite and pooled fund maintenance, as well as the calculation, presentation, and distribution of performance, have been designed in compliance with the GIPS standards and have been implemented on a firm-wide basis. The Japan Large Cap Equity Fund has had a performance examination for the periods from 1 April 2015 to 31 March 2021. The verification and performance examination reports are available upon request.

 

Pudoru Investments is an equity investment manager that invests solely in Japan-based securities.

The Japan Large Cap Equity Fund (the "Fund") seeks to achieve long-term capital appreciation by investing primarily in large-cap equity securities of Japanese issuers. Under normal market conditions, the Fund will invest at least 80% of its net assets (including the amount of any borrowings for investment purposes) in common and preferred stocks of large-capitalization companies. The Fund may from time to time emphasize one or more sectors in selecting its investments, including the financial services sector. The value of the Fund's assets may be adversely affected by economic and social demographics. Japan's population is aging, and the government may have to increase taxes as it spends more on healthcare, which could slow economic growth at a time when Japan has been in a prolonged economic downturn. The Fund may borrow up to 30% of its net asset value. Historically, the Fund's borrowing level has averaged less than 1% of net assets and has never exceeded 10%. Leverage may also magnify losses as well as gains to the extent that leverage is used.

The benchmark is the XYZ Japan Large Cap Index, which is designed to measure the performance of the large-cap segment of the Japanese market. The index is fully invested and includes the reinvestment of dividends.

Valuations are computed and performance is reported in Japanese yen. Policies for valuing investments, calculating performance, and preparing GIPS reports are available upon request.

Gross returns are presented before the deduction of management fees but reflect the deduction of all trading and administrative expenses. Share Class A is used to calculate Fund gross returns. Net returns are calculated by deducting 1/12th of the management fee (0.75% annually, for all share classes) from the monthly gross Fund return. The total expense ratios for Class A and Class I as of the Fund's most recent fiscal year end (31 March 2021) were 1.50% and 1.35%, respectively.

A list of composite and pooled fund descriptions is available upon request.

The inception date of the Fund is 1 April 2011, which is the first day assets were invested in the strategy.

The three-year annualized standard deviation measures the variability of the Fund and the benchmark returns over the preceding 36-month period.

In January 2019, Koh Yuwabara, the Fund's portfolio manager, retired. Yuna Tanaka became the portfolio manager.

GIPS® is a registered trademark of CFA Institute. CFA Institute does not endorse or promote this organization, nor does it warrant the accuracy or quality of the content contained herein.

## SAMPLE 2 POOLED FUND WITH TIME-WEIGHTED RETURNS

**Linker Advisors**
**Juneau Private Placements Bond Fund**
**1 January 2014 to 31 December 2020**

| Year | Fund Gross Return (%) | Benchmark Return (%) | Fund Gross 3-Yr Std Dev (%) | Benchmark 3-Yr Std Dev (%) | Fund Assets (C$ M) | Firm Assets (C$ M) |
|---|---|---|---|---|---|---|
| 2014 | 2.15 | 2.20 | | | 250 | 1,050 |
| 2015 | 7.01 | 6.83 | | | 265 | 1,202 |
| 2016 | 6.12 | 6.07 | 2.82 | 2.80 | 310 | 1,225 |
| 2017 | -2.83 | -3.84 | 3.90 | 4.11 | 301 | 1,227 |
| 2018 | 9.31 | 9.23 | 3.74 | 3.96 | 336 | 1,306 |
| 2019 | 8.52 | 9.74 | 3.47 | 3.76 | 362 | 1,350 |
| 2020 | 4.59 | 2.62 | 2.64 | 2.74 | 404 | 1,411 |

1. Linker Advisors claims compliance with the Global Investment Performance Standards (GIPS®) and has prepared and presented this report in compliance with the GIPS standards. Linker Advisors has not been independently verified.
2. Linker Advisors is a privately owned investment manager registered in all provinces in Canada as a Portfolio Manager and as an Investment Fund Manager in Ontario. The firm primarily provides services to insurance companies, corporations, investment companies, pension and profit-sharing plans, endowments, and state or municipal government entities. Linker Advisors invests in the public equity, private placement, alternative investment, and fixed-income markets both domestically in Canada and throughout the world.
3. The Juneau Private Placement Bond Fund invests in investment-grade, long-term, fixed rate private placement bonds denominated in Canadian dollars, in a variety of industries. Private placement bonds are illiquid investments and have restrictions on transferability. The fund primarily invests in private placement bonds with maturities greater than 10 years that are, therefore, sensitive to changes in interest rates. Investments in the fund are subject to credit risk.
4. The benchmark is the XYZ Canadian Long Duration Fixed Income Index, which consists of Canadian investment-grade corporate bonds with a maturity of 10 years or longer. The fund is valued monthly.
5. Gross fund returns are net of transaction costs and do not reflect the deduction of any pooled fund fees or costs. The management fee is 0.40% per annum. In addition, there is a performance fee of 20% of the excess return over the benchmark return. Performance fees crystalize each 31 December, and the performance fee calculation resets. The total expense ratio was 0.78% as of 31 December 2020. All returns and assets are presented in Canadian dollars.

  

6. The fund inception date is 1 January 2014, which is the date of the first investment.
7. Lists of composite descriptions, limited distribution pooled fund descriptions, and broad distribution pooled funds are available upon request.
8. Policies for valuing investments, calculating performance, and preparing GIPS reports are available upon request.
9. The three-year annualized ex post standard deviation measures the variability of monthly net returns of the fund and benchmark over the preceding 36 months.
10. GIPS® is a registered trademark of CFA Institute. CFA Institute does not endorse or promote this organization, nor does it warrant the accuracy or quality of the content contained herein.

## SAMPLE 3 REAL ESTATE POOLED FUND WITH TIME-WEIGHTED RETURNS

**CMCA Core Commercial Real Estate Fund**
**1 March 2012 to 31 December 2020**

| Calendar Year | Fund Capital Returns Gross (%) | Fund Income Returns Gross (%) | Fund Total Returns Gross (%) | Fund Total Returns Net (%) | Benchmark Returns (%) | Fund Assets ($ M) | Firm Assets ($ M) |
|---|---|---|---|---|---|---|---|
| 3/12–12/12 | 7.33 | 5.25 | 12.59 | 10.94 | 12.05 | 1,370 | 2,385 |
| 2013 | 3.51 | 5.18 | 8.71 | 7.02 | 5.97 | 1,357 | 2,070 |
| 2014 | 0.07 | 4.99 | 5.07 | 3.35 | 2.37 | 1,429 | 1,789 |
| 2015 | (16.36) | 4.78 | (11.54) | (13.14) | (13.13) | 1,611 | 2,451 |
| 2016 | 4.61 | 4.97 | 9.63 | 7.98 | 8.16 | 1,602 | 3,385 |
| 2017 | 3.69 | 4.68 | 8.40 | 6.70 | 7.75 | 1,867 | 5,206 |
| 2018 | 3.34 | 4.50 | 7.85 | 6.13 | 4.99 | 1,203 | 4,820 |
| 2019 | 0.71 | 4.51 | 5.25 | 3.65 | 4.33 | 1,231 | 3,863 |
| 2020 | 3.59 | 4.43 | 8.02 | 6.37 | 5.21 | 1,275 | 3,379 |

1. **Compliance Statement**

   Commercial Mortgage Corporation of America (CMCA) claims compliance with the Global Investment Performance Standards (GIPS®) and has prepared and presented this report in compliance with the GIPS standards. CMCA has been independently verified for the periods 1 January 2014 to 31 December 2020. The verification report is available upon request.

A firm that claims compliance with the GIPS standards must establish policies and procedures for complying with all the applicable requirements of the GIPS standards. Verification provides assurance on whether the firm's policies and procedures related to composite and pooled fund maintenance, as well as the calculation, presentation, and distribution of performance, have been designed in compliance with the GIPS standards and have been implemented on a firm-wide basis. Verification does not provide assurance on the accuracy of any specific performance report.

2. **Definition of the Firm**

   CMCA is an independent investment management firm established in 2011. CMCA invests in and manages commercial properties for our clients with a focus on the United States and Canada.

3. **Fund Description**

   The Core Commercial Real Estate Fund, an open-end fund, invests in Class A commercial properties across the US, including office buildings, retail space, industrial properties, and luxury multi-family dwellings. Key risks of investing in commercial real estate include the following: interest rate risk—an increasing interest rate environment may negatively affect valuations and drive up borrowing costs; liquidity risk—commercial real estate properties are less liquid than many other asset classes, including stocks and bonds. Therefore, it may take longer to sell a property, and property values could move down before we have the chance to realize any unrealized gains; economic risk—commercial property tends to do better when the economy is expanding. During economic downturns, commercial real estate prices may take longer to recover than other asset classes. A moderate level of leverage, typically ranging between 15 and 30%, is used. Leverage magnifies gains and losses. Performance is compared to the XYZ National Core Commercial Property Index.

4. **Inception Date**

   The performance inception date of the fund is 1 March 2012, which is the first day an investment took place.

5. **Benchmark**

   The XYZ National Core Commercial Property Index is an index of geographically diverse commercial properties across the United States. Benchmark returns are a monthly time series of unlevered US commercial properties weighted 25% office, 25% retail, 25% industrial, and 25% multi-family housing. Benchmark returns are calculated quarterly.

6. **Returns and Fees**

   Capital expenditures, tenant improvements, and lease commissions are capitalized, included in the cost of property, and reflected in the capital returns. Gross returns are net of actual transaction costs, custodial, and administrative fees. Net returns are net of actual transaction costs, custodial and administrative fees, and management fees.

  

Net returns are from the institutional (I share) class. All returns and asset values are expressed in US dollars. The management fee schedule for the I share class is 0.80% per annum. The total expense ratio of the I share class was 1.65% as of 31 December 2020.

7. **Ex Post Standard Deviation**

The three-year annualized ex post standard deviation for the fund and benchmark are not presented because fund returns are calculated quarterly and monthly returns are not available.

8. **Valuations**

Investments are valued and returns are calculated quarterly. Internal valuations are determined by applying market discount rates to future projections of gross cash flows and capitalized terminal values over the expected holding period for each asset. To the extent debt is used, the debt is valued separately from the real estate. Properties are externally valued annually. All investments are valued using subjective, unobservable inputs.

9. **Availability**

A list of composite and limited distribution pooled fund descriptions, as well as a list of broad distribution pooled funds, are available on request. Policies for valuing investments, calculating performance, and preparing GIPS Reports are available upon request.

10. **Trademark**

GIPS® is a registered trademark of CFA Institute. CFA Institute does not endorse or promote this organization, nor does it warrant the accuracy or quality of the content contained herein.

## SAMPLE 4 POOLED FUND WITH MONEY-WEIGHTED RETURNS AND SUBSCRIPTION LINE OF CREDIT

**Armor Management**

**Armor Distressed Debt Fund**

**1 July 2012 to 31 December 2020**

| | Since-inception Money-Weighted Returns | | | | | | | | |
|---|---|---|---|---|---|---|---|---|---|
| Year | Fund with Line of Credit (net) (%)[1] | Custom Benchmark (%)[1] | Fund without Line of Credit (net) (%)[2] | Custom Benchmark (%)[2] | Fund Assets (€ M) | Fund Uncalled Committed Capital (€ M) | Total Firm Assets (€ M) | Firm Uncalled Committed Capital (€ M) | Combined Firm Uncalled Committed Capital and Total Firm Assets (€ M) |
| 2020 | 3.50 | 2.90 | 2.50 | 2.32 | 252 | 100 | 11,203 | 1,497 | 12,700 |

[1] Return is for the period from 1 July 2012 (date of the first capital call) through 31 December 2020. See Note 10.

[2] Return is for the period from 16 May 2011 (date of the first fund investment) through 31 December 2020. See Note 10.

  

| Year | Since-Inception Paid in Capital (€ M) | Cumulative Committed Capital (€ M) | Since-Inception Distributions (€ M) | Investment Multiple (TVPI) | Realization Multiple (DPI) | Unrealized Multiple (RVPI) | PIC Multiple (PIC) |
|---|---|---|---|---|---|---|---|
| 2020 | 200 | 300 | 20 | 1.2 | 0.1 | 1.1 | 0.7 |

Armor Management claims compliance with the Global Investment Performance Standards (GIPS®) and has prepared and presented this report in compliance with the GIPS standards. Armor Management has been independently verified for the periods 1 October 2007 through 31 December 2020. The verification report is available upon request. A firm that claims compliance with the GIPS standards must establish policies and procedures for complying with all the applicable requirements of the GIPS standards. Verification provides assurance on whether the firm's policies and procedures related to composite and pooled fund maintenance, as well as the calculation, presentation, and distribution of performance, have been designed in compliance with the GIPS standards and have been implemented on a firm-wide basis. Verification does not provide assurance on the accuracy of any specific performance report.

1. **Definition of the Firm**

   Armor Management is an independent investment management firm established in 2007. Armor Management manages a variety of equity, fixed-income, and balanced assets, primarily for European clients.

2. **Currency**

   Performance is calculated and reported in euros (€).

3. **Pooled Fund Description**

   The Armor Distressed Debt Fund's returns reflect the EUR share class. The fund invests at least 85% of its assets in distressed euro-denominated bonds that have credit ratings of CCC or lower by at least one major credit rating agency. Key risks include widening corporate spreads and defaults, high levels of government debt, and elevated political tensions, which could lead to abrupt changes in monetary policy by the European Central Bank (ECB). A material amount of the fund's investments may be illiquid.

4. **Valuation**

   As of 31 December 2020, 25% of the fund's investments were internally valued. There is no market activity to support valuation for these investments; therefore, valuations are based on the firm's proprietary pricing model using the Euro XYZ Index Swaps yield curve and credit spreads.

5. **Custom Benchmark**

   The custom benchmark return is calculated by applying the investment cash flows of the Armor Distressed Debt Fund to the XYZ Eurozone Distressed Debt Bond Index.

  

The index reflects a portfolio of euro-denominated distressed debt bonds issued in Eurozone countries that generally have credit ratings of CCC or lower from the main rating agencies and are listed on the XYZ platforms.

6. **Returns and Fees**

   Fund returns are net of actual total fund fees and are calculated using the assets of the limited partners. Total fund fees include transaction costs, custodian and other administrative fees, and management fees. The return with the subscription line of credit (LOC) begins at the time of the first capital call from the limited partners which reduces the performance period. This generally will magnify gains or losses in money-weighted returns. The return without the subscription LOC begins with the date of the first fund investment. All returns reflect the deduction of fees and expenses for the subscription LOC.

7. **List of Composite and Pooled Fund Descriptions**

   A list of composite and limited distribution pooled fund descriptions is available upon request.

8. **Policies**

   Armor Management's policies for valuing investments, calculating performance, and preparing GIPS reports are available upon request.

9. **Fee Schedule**

   The fixed management fee for the fund is 0.55% per annum. The total expense ratio as of the most recent year end was 0.86%.

10. **Subscription Line of Credit**

    The fund has a subscription line of credit of €50 million, of which €20 million is outstanding as of 31 December 2020. The subscription line of credit allows the fund to purchase securities without the need to immediately call capital. Interest paid on the line of credit is LIBOR plus 1.5%. The subscription line of credit does not affect the amount of capital called or the committed capital amount.

11. **Trademark**

    GIPS® is a registered trademark of CFA Institute. CFA Institute does not endorse or promote this organization, nor does it warrant the accuracy or quality of the content contained herein.

# APPENDIX C: SAMPLE GIPS ADVERTISEMENTS

## SAMPLE 1 GIPS ADVERTISEMENT WITHOUT PERFORMANCE

**Chippee Asset Management**

Chippee Asset Management is a credit-focused alternative asset manager providing a range of credit services. Chippee Asset Management claims compliance with the Global Investment Performance Standards (GIPS®). GIPS® is a registered trademark of CFA Institute. CFA Institute does not endorse or promote this organization, nor does it warrant the accuracy or quality of the content contained herein.

To obtain GIPS-compliant performance information for the firm's strategies and products, please contact us at info@chippeeassetmanagement.com.

## SAMPLE 2 GIPS ADVERTISEMENT FOR A COMPOSITE WITH TIME-WEIGHTED RETURNS

**Feppy Investments**
**Mid Cap Growth Composite**

### Firm Description

Founded in March 1996, Feppy Investments is an independent investment adviser registered under the Investment Advisers Act of 1940. The firm manages global equity, fixed-income, and balanced strategies, and it was redefined in October 2016 to include both institutional and wrap accounts. Prior to October 2016, the firm included only institutional accounts.

### Investment Approach

The management team believes that equity markets are inefficient and that a bottom-up security selection approach can add alpha. The team does extensive research to identify companies with sustainable growth and high return on invested capital to drive consistent returns. The management team looks for firms that have good business models and are led by management teams with a track record of investing capital wisely.

  

## Annualized Total Returns through December 31, 2020

Inception Date: January 1, 2009

Benchmark: XYZ Mid Cap Growth Index

| Annualized | YTD | 1 Year | 3 Year | 5 Year | 10 Year | Since Inception |
|---|---|---|---|---|---|---|
| Composite gross returns | 12.59% | 12.59% | 2.22% | 8.05% | 10.08% | 14.26% |
| Composite net returns | 11.98% | 11.98% | 1.66% | 7.46% | 9.48% | 13.64% |
| Benchmark returns | 12.11% | 12.11% | 1.80% | 7.24% | 9.37% | 13.42% |

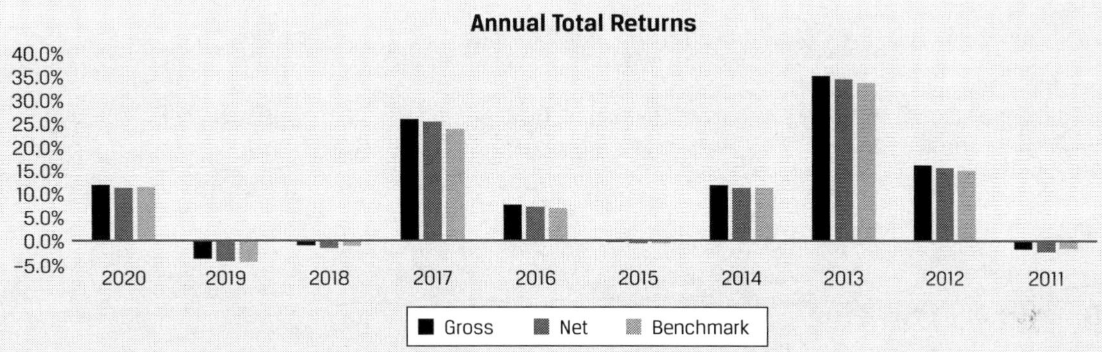


The Mid Cap Growth Composite includes all fully discretionary, institutional accounts managed to the composite strategy. Accounts are primarily invested in US companies whose market capitalization, at time of initial purchase, falls within the capitalization range of the XYZ Mid Cap Growth Index. The stock selection process emphasizes sustainable growth and high return on invested capital. All performance is reported in US dollars.

Feppy Investments claims compliance with the Global Investment Performance Standards (GIPS®). GIPS® is a registered trademark of CFA Institute. CFA Institute does not endorse or promote this organization, nor does it warrant the accuracy or quality of the content contained herein. To obtain a GIPS Composite Report, please call 952-867-5309 or email us at Performance@feppyinvestments.com.

## Other Information

Performance figures are based on historical information and do not guarantee future results. Prospective clients should recognize the limitations inherent in the composite strategy and should consider all information presented by Feppy Investments regarding the firm's investment management capabilities. Registration with the SEC does not imply a certain level of skill or training.



 

## SAMPLE 3 GIPS ADVERTISEMENT FOR A LIMITED DISTRIBUTION POOLED FUND WITH MONEY-WEIGHTED RETURNS

**Bella Management Company**
**CLO Senior Loan Fund**

| Period | Annualized Since-Inception Net MWR (%) | Annualized Since-Inception XYZ Leveraged Loan Bond Index MWR (%) |
|---|---|---|
| 1 Feb 2015 to 30 Sept 2021 | 3.50 | 2.90 |

Bella Management Company claims compliance with the Global Investment Performance Standards (GIPS®). GIPS® is a registered trademark of CFA Institute. CFA Institute does not endorse or promote this organization, nor does it warrant the accuracy or quality of the content contained herein.

### Definition of the Firm

Bella Management Company is an independent investment management firm established in 2007. Bella Management Company manages a variety of pooled fund and separate account equity, fixed-income, and balanced assets.

### Pooled Fund Description

The CLO Senior Loan Fund invests at least 85% of its assets in floating-rate senior secured non-investment-grade bank loans. The fund's benchmark is the XYZ Leveraged Loan Bond Index.

### Performance

Returns are money-weighted returns (MWR) for the period from 1 February 2015 (inception date) through 30 September 2021. The inception date of 1 February 2015 represents the date the first capital call was made. Fund returns reflect the deduction of all fund fees and costs, including asset-based management fees and performance fees. All performance is reported in British pounds.

**To obtain a GIPS Pooled Fund Report, please contact investor relations at +(44) (0) 20 1111-1111 or email us at investorrelations@bellamanagement.com.uk.**

  

## SAMPLE 4 GIPS ADVERTISEMENT FOR A BROAD DISTRIBUTION POOLED FUND

**Ipne Investments**
**Global Bond Fund Fact Sheet**
**Performance as of 12/31/20**

| | A | Adviser | C | Institutional | R |
|---|---|---|---|---|---|
| Share Class Symbol | IBG1Z | DBG2Z | ABG3Z | CBG4Z | RGB5Z |

### Fund Information

| | |
|---|---|
| Fund inception | 1/1/09 |
| Fiscal year end | 12/31 |
| Total net assets (all classes, $B) | $1.43 |
| Number of holdings | 263 |
| Turnover rate (1-year, %) | 68 |
| Average effective duration (years) | 6.34 |
| Weighted average life (years) | 8.73 |
| Management fee (annual, all classes) | 0.65% |
| Total expense ratio (annual, Class A) | 1.00% |

The Global Bond Fund seeks to provide high current income and capital appreciation consistent with a moderate level of risk. The Fund is a core portfolio that invests across global fixed-income markets. The Fund has the flexibility to tactically allocate across sectors, credit qualities, countries, and currencies, allowing for a broadly diversified strategy focused on risk-adjusted returns. The portfolio management team uses both fundamental and quantitative analyses to identify securities with the best relative value.

**Investment Objective:** The Fund seeks to provide shareholders with high current income and capital appreciation consistent with a moderate level of risk.

### Investment Strategy

- Under normal market conditions, the Fund will invest 80% of Fund net assets in debt obligations of issuers located in at least three different countries, which may include the United States.
- The Fund may invest up to 20% of assets in non-investment-grade fixed-income securities.
- The Fund may invest in debt instruments of any maturity and does not seek to maintain a particular dollar-weighted average maturity.
- The Fund generally invests at least 40% of its net assets in debt obligations of foreign governments and companies.
- The Fund may invest in derivatives, including forward contracts, futures contracts, and swap contracts. The use of derivative instruments allows the Fund to obtain net long or short exposure to selected currencies, interest rates, credit risks, and duration risks.
- The Fund is non-diversified, which means that it can invest a greater percentage of its assets in the securities of fewer issuers than can a diversified fund.

  

**Benchmark: XYZ Global Bond Index**

**Base currency of the Fund: USD**

| Risk Measures—3 Years | |
|---|---|
| Sharpe ratio | 0.20 |
| Annualized ex post standard deviation—Net returns, Class A | 2.88 |
| Annualized ex post standard deviation—Benchmark | 2.72 |

## Average Annualized Total Returns

Inception Date: 1/1/2009

| Annualized as of 12/31/20 | YTD* | 1 Year | 3 Year | 5 Year | 10 Year | Since Inception |
|---|---|---|---|---|---|---|
| Net returns, Class A | 4.73% | 4.73% | 0.24% | 1.35% | 2.37% | 3.05% |
| Benchmark | 4.63% | 4.63% | 0.49% | 1.53% | 2.39% | 3.02% |

*Year to date returns are not annualized.

| Annual Returns | 2020 | 2019 | 2018 | 2017 | 2016 | 2015 | 2014 | 2013 | 2012 | 2011 |
|---|---|---|---|---|---|---|---|---|---|---|
| Net returns, Class A | 4.73% | −0.91% | −2.94% | 3.44% | 2.64% | 0.30% | 6.25% | −2.79% | 4.73% | 8.95% |
| Benchmark | 4.63% | −0.54% | −2.48% | 3.55% | 2.66% | 0.57% | 5.95% | −2.02% | 4.23% | 7.86% |

Ipne Investments claims compliance with the Global Investment Performance Standards (GIPS®). Founded in 2010, Ipne Investments invests in global equity and fixed-income securities. GIPS® is a registered trademark of CFA Institute. CFA Institute does not endorse or promote this organization, nor does it warrant the accuracy or quality of the content contained herein.

The benchmark is the XYZ Global Bond Index. This index covers the global investment-grade fixed-rate bond market, including government, credit, and collateralized securities. Indexes are unmanaged and do not incur fees. It is not possible to invest directly in an index.

The total Fund expense ratio is calculated based on the Fund's average net assets during the Fund's most recently completed fiscal year and has not been adjusted for current asset levels. The expense ratio includes operating costs, including administrative, compliance, distribution, management, marketing, shareholder services, and record-keeping fees. Please see the Fund's prospectus for additional details.

The Sharpe ratio is a measure of risk-adjusted performance that measures a portfolio's risk–return efficiency. The risk-free rate used to calculate the Fund's Sharpe ratio is the 90-day

  

Treasury bill. The annualized ex post standard deviation measures the variability of the Class A net returns and the benchmark returns over the preceding 36-month period.

## Primary Risks of the Fund

***An investment in the Fund involves risks, including those described below. There is no assurance that the Fund will achieve its investment objective, and you may lose money.***

*Active Management Risk:* As a result of the investment management team's investment decisions, the Fund could underperform its benchmark index and/or other funds with similar investment objective or strategies.

*Credit Risk:* An issuer of debt securities may fail to make interest payments or repay principal when due, in whole or in part.

*Currency Risk:* Currency rates may fluctuate significantly over short or extended periods of time (i.e., may be extremely volatile), which could result in losses to the Fund if currencies do not perform as the investment manager expects. Changes in currency exchange rates affect the value of the investments that the Fund owns and the Fund's share price.

*Derivatives Risk:* The performance of derivative instruments depends largely on the performance of an underlying currency, security, interest rate or index, and such instruments often have risks similar to the underlying instrument, in addition to other risks. Derivatives involve costs and can create economic leverage in the Fund's portfolio, which may result in significant volatility and cause the Fund to participate in losses (as well as gains) in an amount that significantly exceeds the Fund's initial investment.

*Emerging Market Countries Risk:* The Fund's investments in emerging market countries are subject to all of the risks of foreign investing generally and have additional heightened risks because of a lack of established legal, political, business, and social frameworks to support securities and currency markets.

*Foreign Securities Risk:* Investing in foreign securities typically involves more risks than investing in US securities, including risks associated with (i) internal and external political and economic developments, (ii) trading practices, (iii) availability of information, (iv) limited markets, and (v) currency exchange rate fluctuations and policies.

*High-Yield Debt Securities Risk:* Issuers of lower-rated or "high-yield" debt securities (also known as "junk bonds") are not as strong financially as those issuing higher-credit-quality debt securities. High-yield debt securities are more likely to encounter financial difficulties and are more vulnerable to changes in the relevant economy, such as a recession or a sustained period of rising interest rates, that could affect their ability to make interest and principal payments when due. The prices of high-yield debt securities generally fluctuate more than those of higher credit quality. High-yield debt securities are generally more illiquid (harder to sell).

*Prepayment Risk:* The risk that borrowers will repay a loan more quickly in periods of falling interest rates.

*Sovereign Debt Risk:* The Fund may invest in US and non-US government debt securities ("sovereign debt"). Some investments in sovereign debt, such as US sovereign debt, are considered low risk. Investments in sovereign debt, especially the debt of less developed countries, can involve a high degree of risk, however, including the risk that the governmental entity that controls the repayment of sovereign debt may not be willing or able to repay the principal and/or to pay the interest on its sovereign debt in a timely manner. In the event of default, there may be limited or no legal remedies for collecting sovereign debt and there may be no bankruptcy proceedings through which the Fund may collect all or part of the sovereign debt that a governmental entity has not repaid.

Performance data shown represents past performance and is no guarantee of, and not necessarily indicative of, future results.

  

# APPENDIX D: SAMPLE LISTS

## List of Composite Descriptions

1. **US Large Cap Equity Growth Composite**

   The US Large Cap Equity Growth Composite includes all segregated accounts and pooled funds that invest in large-capitalization US stocks considered to have earnings growth prospects that are superior to that of the average company within the benchmark, the XYZ Large Cap Growth Index. The targeted tracking error is less than 4% per annum.

2. **US Balanced Growth Composite**

   The US Balanced Growth Composite includes all balanced segregated accounts and pooled funds that invest in large-cap US equities and investment-grade bonds, including government, corporate, mortgage-backed, and asset-backed securities. The strategy's investment goal is to provide long-term capital growth and steady income through the creation of a well-diversified portfolio. Although the strategy allows for equity exposure ranging between 50% and 70%, the typical allocation is between 55% and 65%.

3. **Unconstrained Activist UK Equity Composite**

   The Unconstrained Activist UK Equity Composite includes all segregated accounts and pooled funds invested in both listed and unlisted UK equities that pursue an activist investment policy. There is no restriction on the market capitalization of companies held. Portfolios within this composite are highly concentrated, holding approximately 15 securities. Returns may have a lower correlation with the benchmark return than a fully diversified strategy. In times of increased market volatility, the composite characteristics may change significantly, and stock liquidity could be reduced. Because of the strategy's concentrated nature, portfolios tend to have more stock-specific risk than a more diversified strategy. The strategy cannot employ leverage, but portfolios may use both exchange-traded and OTC derivative contracts for efficient portfolio management, which may expose the strategy to counterparty default risk.

4. **Unconstrained Activist UK Equity Carve-Out Composite**

   The Unconstrained Activist UK Equity Carve-Out Composite includes all accounts, including carve-out accounts with allocated cash, and pooled funds invested in both listed and unlisted UK equities that pursue an activist investment policy. There is no restriction on the market capitalization of companies held. Portfolios within this composite are highly concentrated, holding approximately 15 securities. Returns may have a lower correlation with the benchmark return than a fully diversified strategy. In times of increased market volatility, the composite characteristics may change significantly and stock liquidity could be reduced. Because of the strategy's concentrated nature, portfolios tend to have more stock-specific risk than a more diversified strategy. The strategy cannot employ leverage, but portfolios may use both exchange-traded and OTC derivative contracts for efficient portfolio management, which may expose the strategy to counterparty default risk.

5. **UK Liquidity Plus Composite**

   The UK Liquidity Plus Composite includes all segregated accounts and pooled funds invested in a broad range of short-dated interest-bearing deposits, cash equivalents, short-term commercial paper, and other money market investments issued by major UK clearing banks and lending institutions. The strategy has a targeted modified duration of less than one year. The principal investment objectives are preservation of capital, maintenance of liquidity, and provision of yield greater than that available for the benchmark, the three-month risk-free rate. The UK Liquidity Plus strategy differs from more-conventional cash strategies in that it additionally holds short-term commercial paper, which has a greater exposure to credit risk.

6. **Emerging Market High Yield Fixed Income Composite**

   The Emerging Market High Yield Fixed Income Composite includes all pooled funds invested in high-yield debt securities issued by companies outside the OECD. The strategy allows for investment in foreign currency–denominated assets over which the manager has full discretion on hedging. Currency hedging may include instruments such as forward contracts, futures, or foreign exchange derivatives, which may expose the strategy to counterparty default risk. The strategy aims to deliver a total return primarily through income but with some capital growth. High-yield bonds carry increased levels of credit and default risk and are less liquid than government and investment-grade corporate bonds. Investment in less regulated markets carries increased political, economic, and issuer risk. Inherent in fixed-income investing is interest rate and duration risk. Increases to interest rates may negatively affect portfolio valuations. Those risks are magnified when portfolios are invested in bonds with long-dated maturities. The benchmark is the XYZ Emerging Market Bond Index, USD Hedged.

7. **Socially Responsible Investments (SRI) Global Equity Composite**

   The Socially Responsible Investments Global Equity Composite includes all segregated accounts and pooled funds that invest in global equity securities issued by companies that make a positive contribution to society and the environment through sustainable and socially responsible practices. Only securities of companies that meet our proprietary SRI score threshold are allowed. The strategy aims to provide long-term capital appreciation together with a growing income stream through investment in a portfolio of core equity holdings diversified by economic sector, industry group, and geographic business concentration. All foreign currency exposures are fully hedged to US dollars using forward contracts, futures, or foreign exchange derivatives. Foreign exchange forwards and derivatives traded over the counter have counterparty default risk. The SRI process tends to screen out certain companies and sectors, which may result in a more concentrated strategy than a fully diversified strategy. The benchmark is the XYZ World SRI Index.

  

8. **Leveraged Bond Composite**

   The Leveraged Bond Composite includes all segregated accounts in a diversified range of high-yield corporate and government bonds, with the aim of providing investors with a high level of income while seeking to maximize the total return. The accounts are invested in domestic and international fixed-income securities of varying maturities. Inherent in fixed-income investing are interest rate risk and duration risk. Increases to interest rates may negatively affect portfolio valuations. These risks are magnified when portfolios are invested in bonds with long-dated maturities. The strategy also allows investment in exchange-traded and OTC derivative contracts (including, but not limited to, options, futures, swaps, and forward currency contracts) for the purposes of risk, volatility, and currency exposure management. The strategy allows leverage up to but not exceeding twice the value of a portfolio's investments through the use of repurchase financing arrangements with counterparties. Inherent in derivative instrument investments is the risk of counterparty default. Leverage may also magnify losses as well as gains to the extent that leverage is used. The benchmark is the XYZ Global Aggregate Bond Index. The strategy is managed with a maximum tracking error of 6% to 8% per annum.

9. **Global Commodity Equity Composite**

   The Global Commodity Equity Composite includes segregated accounts that globally invest in a diversified range of companies that provide exposure to commodities, energy, and materials. Investment is primarily through the common stock of these companies. Investment directly in raw materials is allowable to a maximum exposure of 10%. Exchange-traded funds and exchange-traded commodity securities up to a maximum 20% exposure are also allowed. The base currency is US dollars, and any or all of the currency risk associated with investments in currencies other than US dollars may be hedged between 0% and 100% using forward contracts, futures, or foreign exchange derivatives. The strategy cannot employ leverage but may use exchange-traded derivative instruments for efficient portfolio management.

   Investments directly or indirectly in commodities may add to portfolio volatility. Global commodity prices can be affected by changes in legislation, national and supra-national policies, and consumer behaviors. In times of commodity price volatility, the liquidity of directly held commodities and the correlation with the broad market can change quickly. Foreign exchange forwards and derivatives traded over the counter have counterparty default risk. In those instances in which currency risk is not hedged, the strategy may be exposed to exchange-rate risk that may create fluctuating gains and/or losses.

10. **Currency Overlay Composite**

    The Currency Overlay Composite includes all segregated accounts invested in a broad range of foreign currency–denominated instruments, such as forward contracts, futures, or foreign exchange derivatives. The principal investment objective is active alpha generation through currency appreciation from movements in exchange rates where the original currency exposures stem from a global or international portfolio. Currency-related investing carries inherent risks related to changes in macroeconomic policy, which can be amplified in the case of emerging markets, where political regime shifts and changes in the control of capital may be more prevalent than in developed markets. In volatile periods, liquidity and correlations between currencies may change expected returns drastically. Foreign exchange forwards and derivatives traded over the counter have counterparty default risk.

**11. Tactical Asset Allocation Overlay Composite**

The Tactical Asset Allocation Overlay Composite includes all segregated accounts in which the investment approach is designed to profit from the increase/decrease in exposure to one or more asset classes. Managing the collateral is part of the strategy. The accounts in this composite are hedged to euros using forward contracts, futures, or foreign exchange derivatives. Allocation shifts are typically implemented via long and short futures, options, and swaptions. This strategy allows leverage up to but not exceeding 180% of each account's value. Accounts are expected to have an investment exposure above 100%. Inherent in derivative instruments is the risk of counterparty default. A leveraged account may result in large fluctuations in value and entails a high degree of risk, including the possibility of substantial losses.

**12. Covered Call Writing Overlay Composite**

The Covered Call Writing Overlay Composite is composed of all segregated accounts for which covered call writing is conducted to generate additional income for an underlying large-cap US equity portfolio. The strategy seeks to generate monthly option premium income while protecting against downward moves in the underlying portfolio through selling covered calls with a monthly duration on US equities held in the underlying portfolio, either at the money or slightly out of or in the money. The use of derivatives, such as equity options, can involve a high degree of financial risk because a relatively small movement in the price of the underlying security or benchmark may result in an unexpected or disproportionately large movement, unfavorable or favorable, in the price of the derivative instrument. The strategy does not use leverage.

**13. Asian Market Neutral Composite**

The Asian Market Neutral Composite includes all segregated accounts with a market-neutral strategy that invests in publicly traded companies with market capitalizations greater than $500 million in developed and emerging Asian markets. The strategy's principal objective is to outperform the return of the three-month US Treasury Bill by at least 1 percentage point per annum. The strategy uses a risk-controlled quantitative screening and optimization process that invests at least 85% of the net asset value in long equity positions and at least 85% of the net asset value in short equity positions. The strategy's long portion overweights those securities that have been quantitatively identified as potentially exhibiting superior and sustainable earnings growth compared with the market. The strategy's short portion consists of securities that have been identified as having inferior growth prospects or that may also be adversely affected by either specific events or momentum considerations. The strategy may engage in currency hedging using instruments such as forward contracts, futures, or foreign exchange derivatives.

  

The Asian Market Neutral strategy seeks to balance exposures between long and short positions so that broad market movements are neutralized. In certain market conditions, the investment process behind the strategy can give rise to unmatched country, sector, industry, market capitalization, and/or style bias exposures in the portfolio. Investment in less regulated markets carries increased political, economic, and issuer risk. Foreign exchange forwards and derivatives traded over the counter have counterparty default risk. This active trading strategy involves significantly greater stock turnover when compared to passive strategies.

14. **Value-Added Asian Real Estate Composite**

    The Value-Added Asian Real Estate Composite consists of all portfolios managed within the value-added investment strategy. The strategy has an equal focus on income and capital appreciation. The strategy invests in multi-family, office, industrial, and retail property types within developed Asian markets that require correction or mitigation of the investments' operating, financial, redevelopment, and/or management risk(s). A level of leverage ranging between 60% and 80% is used. Leverage may magnify losses as well as gains to the extent that it is used. All foreign currency exposures are fully hedged to Singapore dollars using forward contracts, futures, or foreign exchange derivatives. Foreign exchange forwards and derivatives traded over the counter have counterparty default risk. Real estate investments are generally illiquid.

15. **Leveraged US Direct Lending Senior Composite**

    The Leveraged US Direct Lending Senior Composite includes all pooled funds that primarily invest in directly originated, US dollar–denominated first lien and unitranche loans to high-quality US middle market companies. Middle market companies are generally defined as having $10 million to $150 million of EBITDA and are primarily backed by private equity sponsors. The strategy seeks to generate higher levels of income and total return than the broadly syndicated leveraged loan market, with less volatility. The strategy uses leverage to increase returns. The target level of leverage is 100% with a maximum allowable level of 150%. Directly originated loans are generally illiquid and carry increased liquidity risk. Leverage may magnify gains as well as losses to the extent that it is used. Funds in the composite are structured as drawdown funds, whereby the firm has control over capital calls and distributions.

## Terminated Composites

1. **US Core Equity Composite**

    The US Core Equity Composite includes all segregated accounts and pooled funds managed to a growth at a reasonable price (GARP) strategy through investment in a high-quality, focused portfolio of domestic, large-capitalization stocks expected to generate returns above the XYZ Large Cap Index over a market cycle. A quantitative screening process is used together with fundamental research to construct portfolios. The strategy is managed with a maximum tracking error of 4% per annum. Quantitative-driven investment screening relies on historical stock correlations, which can be adversely affected during periods of severe market volatility. The composite terminated in March 2018.

  

## Limited Distribution Pooled Fund Descriptions

### Stable Growth 2022 Fund

The investment objective of the Stable Growth 2022 Fund is to realize stable capital growth consistent with strict risk control, while ensuring sufficient liquidity is available for investment. This is a medium/low-level risk product with an expected moderate level of income. Client-invested assets will be locked up until 31 December 2022; no redemption is allowed during this period. The Fund aims to invest in treasury bonds, municipal bonds, central bank bills, medium and small enterprise private bonds, commercial paper, medium-term notes, and asset-backed securities, as well as other money market funds, bond funds, or bank deposit products, all of which are issued in China's domestic market. This Fund may also invest in products such as bank-issued wealth management products and specific asset management plans (SAMPs) issued by another fund management house or securities house. The Fund may invest in other SAMPs under management by our firm or by our parent company, ABC Fund House, with possible related-party transactions involved. Asset allocation among the investment instruments can vary from 0% to 100% of total fund assets. The Fund is benchmarked against the three-month Financial Institution Deposit Rate + Net Interest Income (NII). The NII is greater than 1% and less than 10%, as stated in the subscription legal document. Interest rate risk is a primary risk of the fund. When interest rates rise, debt security prices generally fall.

### Contrarian Core Trust Fund

The Contrarian Core Trust Fund seeks to provide total returns that are composed of current income and long-term capital appreciation. To achieve this objective, the investment team strives to capitalize on out-of-favor stocks that the market has undervalued. The team uses both quantitative and fundamental research to select investments from the large universe of equity securities. Under normal circumstances, the Fund invests at least 80% of its net assets in equity securities of US companies that have large market capitalizations that the investment management team believes are undervalued and have the potential for long-term growth and current income. The Fund may also invest up to 20% of its net assets in foreign securities. The Fund may invest directly in foreign securities or indirectly through American depositary receipts. Investing in foreign securities typically involves more risks than investing in US securities, including risks associated with (i) internal and external political and economic developments, (ii) trading practices, (iii) availability of information, (iv) limited markets, and (v) currency exchange rate fluctuations and policies. The Fund may from time to time emphasize one or more sectors in selecting its investments, including the financial services sector and the information technology and technology-related sectors. The Fund's benchmark is the XYZ Large Cap Index. The Fund's principal risks are active management risk, depositary receipt risk, issuer risk, market risk, sector risk, and value securities risk.

  

## Global Liquidity Relative Value Fund

The Global Liquidity Relative Value Fund invests in long and short positions in government securities of the United States and other developed markets, US agency securities, mortgage-backed securities issued or guaranteed by US government-sponsored enterprises or agencies, and derivatives. The Fund may also invest in long and short positions in government securities of select emerging market countries. It seeks to maximize total return on a risk-adjusted basis. Investment risks include currency fluctuation, political and economic changes, and emergent financial markets. Fixed-income derivatives may be used, including bond futures, swaps, and options. These investments are both exchange-traded and traded over the counter with approved counterparties, which minimizes liquidity risk. They are used for three purposes: timing to catch immediate market moves, providing the cheapest means of gaining or reducing interest rate and currency exposure, and creating an asymmetrical risk–return profile during times of heightened volatility. Derivatives usage exposes the Fund to risks different from, and potentially greater than, the risks associated with investing directly in securities and may result in additional loss, which could be greater than the cost of the derivative. The Fund may use leverage by purchasing securities on margin or by entering into repurchase agreements and credit agreements. The Fund may pledge its securities to borrow additional funds or otherwise obtain leverage for investment or other purposes. Leverage reflects the greater of the absolute value of the long or short positions of the Fund divided by the Fund's net asset value. The Fund is generally levered in the range of 10 to 12 times. The use of leverage may result in large fluctuations in the Fund's value and entails a high degree of risk, including the possibility of substantial losses.

## European Real Estate Fund

The European Real Estate Fund is a core, diversified real estate fund that invests in European commercial real estate that exhibits strong and stable cash flow and the potential for long-term capital growth. This Fund is offered only to professional investors. The European Real Estate Fund is a low-leveraged fund that invests primarily in industrial, retail, and office properties located across Europe. The focus is on properties that have a steady income and properties that, through development or redevelopment, have the potential to achieve future positive returns. The target level of leverage is 50% with a maximum allowable level of 60%. A leveraged fund may result in large fluctuations in the value of the Fund and entails a high degree of risk, including the possibility of substantial losses. Real estate investments are generally illiquid, and the investment outlook may change given the availability of credit or other financing sources. Because of the illiquidity, withdrawals could take some time to execute. The Fund is benchmarked to the XYZ Commercial Real Estate Index.

## European Private Equity Fund

The European Private Equity Fund is a fund-of-private equity funds that invests in European small- and mid-cap buyout, growth, and restructuring funds. This Fund requires a minimum commitment of €10 million, and is offered only to professional investors who can withstand a total loss of their initial investment. Capital calls are dependent on investment progress and subscription amount. The Fund uses leverage. The target level of leverage is 40% with a maximum allowable level of 60%. A leveraged fund may incur large fluctuations in value and entails a high degree of risk, including the possibility of substantial losses. Private equity investments are generally illiquid, and the investment outlook may change given the availability of credit or other financing sources. The Fund's value is expected to follow a J-curve, so that in the first years the Fund value is expected to be below booking value. Generally, the Fund's returns are generated after a period of five to seven years, when selling the investments. Investors should have an investment horizon of at minimum 7 to 10 years.

## Insurance-Linked Securities (ILS) Fund

The Insurance-Linked Securities (ILS) Fund invests globally in high-yield insurance-linked bonds (cat bonds) whose return depends on the occurrence of specific insured events, such as natural catastrophic events. The investments are broadly diversified across various insured risks (wind, earthquake, wildfire, and other natural disasters) and geographic locations. Besides investments in cat bonds, the Fund may also invest up to 30% of assets in illiquid, direct private reinsurance contracts (collateralized reinsurance, or CRI). CRI investments are illiquid and typically cannot be disposed of prior to their expiration (minimum investment period of one year). Because of the nature of ILS investments, they are uncorrelated with the typical capital market risks. The issuer and counterparty risks are fully hedged by means of risk-free collateral. The Fund is benchmarked to the XYZ Cat Bond Index.

## Short Duration Fund

The Short Duration Fund is a private placement fund whose objective is to provide current income while preserving capital. The strategy primarily invests in fixed-income securities issued or guaranteed by the US government or by its respective agencies. The Fund may also invest in mortgage-backed securities, including collateralized mortgage obligations, corporate debt, and other US dollar–denominated obligations issued in the United States by non-US banks and corporations. The Fund may invest up to 10% of assets in non-investment-grade securities. A portion of the Fund's assets may be invested in illiquid securities that do not have a readily available market. The Fund may invest in certain types of derivatives such as futures and options. .The principal risks of the Fund are active management risk, market risk, interest rate risk, credit risk, derivative instruments risk, counterparty risk, extension risk, prepayment risk, and high-yield debt securities risk. The Fund is benchmarked to the XYZ Short-Term US Government Credit Index.

## 2018 Venture Capital Fund

The 2018 Venture Capital Fund seeks long-term capital appreciation by acquiring minority interests in early-stage technology companies. The Fund invests in technology companies in Europe,

  

Asia Pacific, and emerging markets. European venture investments are more concentrated than in the other regions and are focused on a few high-quality companies. Exit opportunities include IPOs, trade sales, and secondary sales. Opportunities in China and India will be targeted for investment, and an allocation to Chinese high-tech will be at least 10% of the invested capital over the Fund's life. International venture capital investments are generally illiquid and are subject to currency risk. If investment opportunities and/or exit strategies become limited, the life of the fund may be extended, and capital calls and distributions may be delayed. The Fund is benchmarked to the XYZ Venture Capital Index.

## 2016 Buyout Strategy Fund of Funds

The 2016 Buyout Strategy Fund of Funds includes primary and secondary partnership investments with strategies focused on leveraged and growth-oriented buyouts, primarily in the United States. Managers of partnerships are expected to focus on reducing costs, preparing companies for downturn, and providing operational improvement rather than financial engineering. Investments may be in small, medium, and large buyout partnerships, aiming to make selective commitments diversifying across stages, industries, and vintage years. Secondary deals take advantage of distressed primary partnership sales, providing access to an increased mix of assets. The underlying funds are leveraged 100% to 300%. A leveraged fund may result in large fluctuations in value and entails a high degree of risk, including the possibility of substantial losses. Private equity investments are illiquid and, therefore, if investment opportunities and/or exit strategies become limited, the Fund's life may be extended, and capital calls and distributions may be delayed.

## Value-Added Strategy Closed-End Real Estate Commingled Fund

The Value-Added Strategy Closed-End Real Estate Commingled Fund is managed using a value-added investment strategy with a focus on both income and appreciation. Portfolio management intends to invest in properties located in major markets within the United States with higher operational risk than traditional property types. The target level of leverage is 60% with a maximum allowable level of 70%. A leveraged fund may result in large fluctuations in the value of the fund and entails a high degree of risk, including the possibility of substantial losses. Real estate investments are generally illiquid, and the investment outlook may change given the availability of credit or other financing sources. If investment opportunities or exit strategies become limited, the Fund's life may be extended, and capital calls and distributions may be delayed.

## List of Broad Distribution Pooled Funds

1. High Yield Fund
2. New Jersey Municipal Fund
3. Quantitative Core Fund
4. Small Cap Value Fund
5. US Treasury Index Fund
6. World Allocation Fund

## Broad Distribution Pooled Fund Descriptions

### US Fixed Income Fund

The Fund is designed to maximize total return by investing in a portfolio of investment-grade intermediate- and long-term debt securities. The Fund will primarily invest in corporate bonds, US Treasuries, other US government and agency securities, and asset-backed, mortgage-related, and mortgage-backed securities. The Fund will invest at least 80% of its assets in bonds and up to 20% in cash and cash equivalents. The Fund is subject to general market risk, interest rate risk, credit (issuer and counterparty) risk, and liquidity risk. General market risk is the risk that the value of the securities owned by the Fund may underperform because of factors affecting particular industries or securities markets generally. Interest rate risk is the risk the values of bonds will change by changes in interest rates. If rates increase, the value of bonds declines in general. Credit risk is the risk the value of investments may change because of changes in creditworthiness of issuers of debt securities and default of counterparties in investment transactions. Liquidity risk is the risk the Fund may have a loss when it sells securities to raise cash for redemption requests by other shareholders.

### Global Equity Market Neutral Fund

The Fund takes long and short positions in different securities, selecting from a universe of global stocks with similar characteristics to those in the XYZ World Equity Index. The Fund purchases securities that it believes are undervalued and sells short securities that it believes are overvalued. The long and short positions are matched in order to limit exposure to macroeconomic factors. Derivatives may be used as substitutes for securities in which the Fund can invest. Specific risks include: leverage risk, which can increase market exposure and magnify losses; derivatives risk, which is the risk that losses may be greater than investing directly in the underlying securities; and short selling risk, which is the risk that in selling borrowed securities, the short seller may be unable to purchase them at a price lower than the price at which they were sold, which could result in unlimited losses. Leverage is not expected to exceed more than 200% of total net assets.

  

## Global Absolute Return Fund

The Fund seeks to provide total returns and maintain a relatively low correlation with traditional asset classes. The Fund may buy or sell stocks and bonds across various countries and industry sectors and applies an active currency strategy. The Fund makes use of derivatives, including swaps, futures, and forwards, in implementing its strategies. In addition to market, interest rate, credit, and currency risks, alternative investing may include complicated investment techniques that could result in greater volatility and loss. The Fund may use leverage. Leverage is not expected to exceed more than 200% of total net assets. Leverage may result in large fluctuations in the Fund's value and entails a high degree of risk, including the possibility of substantial losses. The Fund uses certain derivatives that involve counterparty risk. Counterparty risk is the risk that the counterparty may fail to fulfill its obligation under the contract, resulting in losses to the Fund. Short selling risk is the risk that securities sold short (borrowed) may rise significantly in price, resulting in unlimited losses when purchased to close the position in the security.

## US Small Cap Equity Fund

The Fund aims to achieve long-term capital growth by investing in US companies with market capitalization of less than $2 billion. The Fund aims to outperform the XYZ US Small Cap Equity Index. The Fund invests at least 80% of its assets in equities of small US companies. These companies are similar in size to those that constitute the bottom 20% by market capitalization of the North American equity markets. The Fund may also invest in other equities, equivalent securities, and cash. The Fund's base currency is the euro. Specific risk factors include the following: The Fund is unhedged, and changes in exchange rates could result in losses relative to the euro. Small-cap equity prices can be more volatile than larger-cap stocks and carry more risk. In difficult market conditions, the Fund may be unable to sell a security for full value or at all. This scenario could affect performance and could cause the Fund to defer or suspend redemptions of its shares.

## Global Credit Income Fund

The Global Credit Income Fund's investment objective is to (i) provide income and capital growth over the long term by investing in bonds issued by governments and companies globally and (ii) invest at least two-thirds of its assets in investment-grade bonds and high-yield bonds issued by governments, government agencies, supra-nationals, and companies globally, including emerging markets. The Fund allocates across a range of global credit sectors with a bottom-up approach while managing duration and currency risk. The Fund targets a portfolio-weighted average duration range of three to five years. The Fund may use derivatives with the aim of achieving investment gains, portfolio efficiency, and/or reducing risk. Specific risk factors include the following: Mortgage or asset-backed securities may not receive in full the amounts owed to them by underlying borrowers. The counterparty to a derivative or other contractual agreement may be unable to honor its commitments, potentially creating a loss for the Fund. A derivative may not perform as expected and may cause the Fund to lose as much or more than the amount invested. Leverage is not expected to exceed more than 200% of total net assets. A leveraged fund may result in large value fluctuations and entails a high degree of risk, including the possibility of substantial losses. High-yield bonds generally carry greater market, credit, and liquidity risk. A rise in interest rates generally causes bond prices to fall.

## Diversified Equity Fund

The Fund aims to generate an absolute return above the UK inflation rate over an economic cycle (typically five years) at a risk level lower than equity markets as represented by the XYZ Global Broad Market Index (the benchmark). The Fund may invest in a broad range of asset classes including equities, bonds, infrastructure, property, commodities, and absolute return strategies. Investment in these asset classes may be made through a wide range of investment vehicles including transferable securities, derivatives, deposits, collective investment schemes, money market instruments, and cash. The Fund may take long and short positions in markets via derivatives contracts. Specific risk factors include the following: The Fund may be concentrated in a limited number of geographical regions, industry sectors, markets, or individual positions. This may result in large changes in the Fund's value, either up or down. Emerging markets generally carry greater political, legal, counterparty, and operational risk. As infrastructure and property assets are unlisted, the strategy is subject to liquidity risk, specifically the risk of low price discovery and/or the ability to transact in the market freely. Derivatives carry the risk of reduced liquidity and increased volatility in adverse market conditions. Use of derivatives will result in the Fund being leveraged, where the potential for losses exceeds the amount invested. Leverage is not expected to exceed more than 300% of total net assets.

## UK Gilt Fund

The Fund aims to achieve long-term capital growth and income by investing primarily in UK government securities across all maturities. The Fund may also hold exposure to sterling credit bonds and non-sterling bonds (hedged back to British pounds). The Fund targets a portfolio-weighted average duration range of between three and six years. The Fund may use derivatives to achieve the investment objective, reduce risk, or manage the Fund more efficiently. Specific risk factors include the following: The counterparty to a derivative or other contractual agreement may be unable to honor its commitments to the Fund, potentially creating a loss for the Fund. Derivatives usage exposes the Fund to risks different from, and potentially greater than, the risks associated with investing directly in securities and may result in additional losses, which could be greater than the cost of the derivative. A decline in an issuer's financial health could cause the value of its bonds to fall or become worthless. When interest rates rise, bond values generally fall; this risk increases the longer the investment's maturity. Leverage is not expected to exceed more than 200% of total net assets. A leveraged fund may result in large value fluctuations and entails a high degree of risk, including the possibility of substantial losses.

  

## Asian High Yield Fund

The Fund invests in a diversified mix of high-yield fixed-income securities issued by Asian entities or their subsidiaries. The Fund aims to outperform the XYZ Asian High Yield Index. The Fund applies both top-down and bottom-up investment approaches, targeting duration, credit, and allocation. The Fund targets to be within 0.5 years (+/–) of the benchmark weighted average duration. Securities can be denominated in US dollars as well as the various Asian currencies, and the Fund focuses on securities rated below BBB–. The Fund may invest up to 30% of its assets in asset-backed, mortgage-backed, distressed, and defaulted securities, and it may invest up to 20% in derivatives. Specific risk factors include market risks peculiar to Asian bond markets, high-yield credit risk, structured product risk, and emerging market risk. Currency, interest rate, and credit risks are general risk factors to consider. As a result of liquidity risk, the Fund may have a loss when it sells securities to raise cash for redemption requests by other shareholders.

## European Equity Fund

The Fund aims to invest in high-quality companies in well-structured, growing industries, focusing on long-term growth. The Fund aims to invest in between 40 and 50 companies, outperform its benchmark (the XYZ European Equity Index) by 250 bps to 300 bps per year, and achieve a target tracking error of 3% to 6% per annum. In selecting investments for the Fund, the portfolio manager considers the results of a top-down country- and sector-specific analysis while using a fundamental bottom-up approach to stock selection relative to the benchmark. Specific risk factors include investments in illiquid securities, which include securities yet to list, IPOs, or securities undergoing corporate actions that limit trading. Especially in times of economic distress, the Fund may incur greater losses than if the Fund had been invested in liquid securities.

## European Bond Fund

The Fund combines a top-down and bottom-up investment process that allocates risk across sectors and maturities, focused on well-diversified investment-grade Eurozone fixed-income securities. The Fund is benchmarked against the XYZ Euro Aggregate Bond Index. It aims to invest in 100 to 125 issuers to generate income and capital gains through investments predominantly in A+ and above rated corporate bonds. The Fund targets a portfolio-weighted average duration range of between three and five years. Specific risk factors include concentration risk, sovereign risk, and risks associated with investment in securitized debt.

## World Allocation Fund

The Fund seeks to achieve its investment objective by investing in other mutual funds for which the firm is the investment manager ("underlying funds"). The Fund is considered a "fund of funds." These underlying funds represent a variety of asset classes and investment styles.

Through investments in these underlying funds, the Fund invests in issuers from several different countries. As a result, the Fund normally will have approximately 35% to 55% of its net assets allocated to non-US investments, including emerging market countries. The target asset class allocation of the Fund is 60% to equity investments, 30% to fixed-income securities and money market instruments, and 10% to alternative investments. The portfolio management team will rebalance the asset class allocations and Fund's investments based on the results of a proprietary quantitative model and continuous monitoring of market conditions. When market conditions dictate a more defensive strategy, the Fund or an underlying fund may temporarily hold cash or cash equivalents. In that case, the Fund's allocated holdings may be significantly different from its target allocations. As a result, the Fund may not achieve its investment objective. Given the scope of the Fund, it is subject to numerous types of risks including, but not limited to, affiliated fund risk, allocation risk, alternative investment allocation risk, counterparty risk, derivatives risk, equity security risk, fixed-income security risk, foreign exposure risk, quantitative model risk, and sovereign debt risk. For more information concerning the underlying funds of this Fund and their respective risks, please request a current prospectus.

  

Made in the USA
Monee, IL
13 September 2026

62975575R00079